the **modern** garden

jane brown

the
modern
garden

with special photography by
Sofia Brignone and Alan Ward

with 312 illustrations 156 in colour

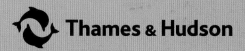
Thames & Hudson

contents

introduction   **6**

chapterone

Return to **the Oracles**   **14**

De Stijl   **16**

Le Corbusier and the French
   Modernists   **19**

Erich Mendelsohn (1887–1953)   **25**

Paul Klee (1887–1940)   **29**

masterworkone   **30**
Fletcher **Steele**
   Naumkeag, Stockbridge,
   Massachusetts, USA

masterworktwo   **38**
Gabriel **Guevrekian**
   Villa Noailles, Hyères,
   France

chaptertwo

Britain **in the 1930s**   **48**

Bentley Wood (1934–38)   **55**

Constructive art and the
   modern garden   **58**

Christopher Nicholson   **61**

St Ann's Hill, Chertsey (1936–38)   **62**

Christopher Tunnard (1910–79)   **65**

Plans Analysis   **68**

masterworkthree   **72**
Walter **Gropius**
   Lincoln, Massachusetts, USA

chapterthree

America   **80**

The East Coast: landfall   **81**

Garrett Eckbo (b. 1910)   **85**

Thomas Church (1902–78)   **88**

The modern garden in prairie
   and desert   **94**

masterworkfour   **98**
Dan **Kiley**
   Miller House, Columbus,
   Indiana, USA

masterworkfive   **106**
Roberto **Burle Marx**
   Brazil

chapterfour

Dressing the
Modern Garden   114

Designers' plants   120

John Nash (1893–1977):
   the modern artist-plantsman   126

Designer's plant lists   130

Concrete and other modern
   materials   134

The wild garden and
   the 'Stockholm School'   134

masterworksix   136
Russell **Page**
   Villa Silvio Pellico,
   Turin, Italy

masterworkseven   142
Mien **Ruys**
   Dedemsvaart, Overijssel,
   Netherlands

chapterfive

Post-war Europe:
a Second Flowering   154

Post-war Britain   156

Post-war Denmark   162

masterworkeight   166
Pietro **Porcinai**
   Villa Il Roseto,
   Florence, Italy

masterworknine   176
Arne **Jacobsen**
   St Catherine's College,
   Oxford, UK

chaptersix

The Modern Garden:
to be continued?   184

masterworkten   194
Luis **Barragán**
   Mexico

masterworkeleven   200
Ludwig **Gerns**
   Hanover, Germany

Notes   209
Selected Reading   216
Gazetteer   217
Picture credits   218
Index   220
Copyright   224

introduction

the 20th century's
ideal of private space

This is an analytic rather than encyclopaedic treasure hunt – the treasure in question is that lost child of the international modern movement in art, architecture and design: the modern garden. The search entails returning to the oracles of the Bauhaus pioneers, following their exodus from Europe to temporary haven in Britain during the 1930s, and then to their more permanent landfall in America. The modern garden achieved stature in America, so much so that it tended to become an interpretation of the modern landscape (an elephantiasis that is carefully examined in chapter 3), and it was re-exported to a rather mystified Europe in the 1950s. Within a decade it was dead, mainly through misunderstanding, and a smothering in historic revivals and rampantly eclectic postmodernism.

The pity is that the modern garden encompassed in theory and practice ecological empathy, flexibility in maintenance, lack of expensive pretence, and avoidance of finite materials and harmful substances – all of which gardeners, architects and designers have been clamorously demanding, largely in vain, for the last forty years. The theory of the

Cranbrook Academy, Bloomfield Hills, Michigan. This working place for creative people was masterminded, conceived and designed by Eliel Saarinen in 1925. Refuge and home for the Saarinens and the sculptor Carl Milles, it reflects their love for their native northlands and traditions.

modern garden was never carefully codified by any latter-day Humphry Repton, nor have the gardens that were made survived well. The modern garden is elusive, but it was more than merely a dream: it served to focus some of the twentieth century's great ideas.

The title, *The Modern Garden*, is carefully chosen, but requires some justification. *The* is intentionally specific, and *Modern* is just as the dictionary defines it, i.e. of the recent present, and most emphatically 'not antiquated'. But Modern, with a capital M, suggests the International Modern Movement or High Modern Movement in architecture in the first half of the twentieth century. Though sometimes called 'modernism', 'isms' are out of favour here (one of the freedoms of garden history being from the fetters of architectural criticism).

However, both 'international' and 'movement', purposely omitted from my title, are both difficult concepts in the realm of gardens. The garden history of the world is encased in cultural styles, in national traditions, the very essences of the Mogul garden or the Italian garden being compressions of those cultures and traditions. A garden is also dependent upon geography, upon soil and climate, and ultimately and most vitally upon the microclimatic variations set up within its boundaries: how can a garden be international? Nationalism – a cause of the First World War, and a sign of the burgeoning extremism of Germany under Adolf Hitler's National Socialist Workers' Party – was a dangerous word, so the Marxist overtones of Internationalism seemed preferable. These political connections can never be entirely erased – the modern pioneers undoubtedly saw their designs as suitable for life in the 'global village' that our Earth has apparently become, but they cannot be blamed for failing to foretell shifts of political preference. The word 'international' is now attached to the modern movement by historians to denote a period in its twentieth-century context (particularly the 1930s, when young idealists joined the International Brigades during the Spanish Civil War). To ask whether internationalism is either desirable or possible in gardens is implicit in the chapters that follow.

The idea of a movement is not solely the prerogative of modern design, but it is the word that weighs most heavily upon the page, as upon the twentieth-century, and no cultural activity was so aptly named: it suggests not only movements in art or design, but the movement of ideas from the backwoods of Europe to the New World; or the physical movement of people, often against their will or because of imminent danger. But equally important here is the mechanical means of movement, the modern passion for travelling that distinguishes the twentieth century, the century of cars and aeroplanes, and of the speeded-up perceptions and possibilities that they have brought. The movement of people and ideas is the antithesis of settlement, and settlement is the prime requirement for the making of a garden. Undoubtedly some reactions against the speed of modern life centred upon the garden, which came to be regarded as the last refuge of the quiet past. Finally, there is the inevitable nature of gardens to grow, change and deteriorate. Growth and neglect, changes in circumstances and consequent decay, may mean that the modern garden is elusive, but does not mean that it was never there at all.

The word *Garden* in my title is also carefully emphatic: it implies the use and enjoyment of a private space, within similar parameters to those that we apply to our private lives, allowing room for friends and close and known local communities. There is a definite line to be drawn between the meaning of the word garden, and that other word, landscape, with which it is so persistently confused. The source of this confusion is part of the story of the modern garden, when its theory was appropriated by landscape architects wishing to rejuvenate their profession, as explained in chapter 3. There is no high-horticultural or 'gardening' requirement, for the modern garden is as flexible in its planting as in other ways, but certain moods and perceptions of planting are necessary and these are explored in chapter 4.

The modern movement in architecture and design was born of an impatience with the past, and an angry rejection of history. In our calendar, it is as if the twentieth century made a promising start, and then blundered so appallingly into the First World War, that it was resolved to begin all over again. The architect Walter Gropius, the prime mover, was a patriotic German and intensely proud of his family's past and achievements: he was awarded the Iron Cross for his bravery in the War, and was completely devastated and shamed by Germany's defeat in 1918, a defeat that he felt wrenched him from his happy youth, destroyed his marriage and thereby deprived him of his children.[1] He dedicated himself to changing everything – one can almost hear him spitting 'All the old stuff was out', as he jettisoned both his own and his architecture's entire and once-beloved past.[2] Another of the 'oracles' of chapter one, the sculptor Naum Gabo, issued his *Realistic Manifesto* in 1920 from post-revolutionary Moscow, 'across the ashes and cindered homes of the past. Before the gates of the vacant future'. The Manifesto was to fire the modern mind: as an artist Gabo rejected 'colour as a pictorial element', descriptive line, pictorial and plastic spatial forms, mass as a sculptural necessity, and the static rhythms of sculpture and painting, replacing them with kinetic, i.e. moving perceptions. The Manifesto ended with passionate anger:

Today is the deed.
We will account for it tomorrow.
The past we are leaving behind as carrion.
The future we leave to the fortune-tellers.
We take the present day.[3]

Another of the oracles, Erich Mendelsohn, served on both the Russian and Western fronts in the First World War, sketching in his trench to bolster his instinct to survive, knowing that self-preservation was a desperately aggressive state of mind, and chanting his mantra – 'One must love life if one is to think "live", one must understand life in order to love it'.[4] Having survived, Mendelsohn assumed a potent energy, exhibiting his trench drawings and devoting himself to his second chance.

When the young Walter Segal applied to study at the Dessau Bauhaus in 1926 with Gropius's encouragement, he enquired whether the history of architecture would be taught, but Gropius declared 'that in a modern school that was not necessary'.[5] This rejection of history, it must be emphasized, was more deeply felt than Le Corbusier's chanting of 'The Styles are a Lie': it was not merely the styles, but the whole of society that required a clean slate. In the minds of the modern movement pioneers the old world, ground into Flanders mud, dashed in the slaughter of the Russian front, had to go. In 1920, the year of Gabo's *Realistic Manifesto*, there was no going back, nowhere to go back to. Gardens above all belonged to a tainted aristocracy – in every way 1920 was the standing start.

However, if history on the continental scale was shameful, the individual experience, especially amongst the pioneers, reflected a renewed love of nature and the countryside. A love of nature is also a basic tenet of the modern movement, although too often immediately assumed to be in the manner of the English landscape style or the Picturesque. The advent of modern design in Britain coincided with the publication of Christopher Hussey's *The Picturesque* (1927) and the retrieval of the English landscape style from Victorian disfavour, which prompted Dorothy Stroud's work on Lancelot 'Capability' Brown. The British intelligentsia, especially the gentlemanly editors of the taste-making *Architectural Review* and *Country Life* magazine, were so enchanted by the eighteenth century in general and Brown in particular, 'Lady Nature's second husband', that no notion of 'nature' or a native landscape could be comprehended outside a landscaped park. Thus the *englischer Garten*, *jardin anglais*, became associated with the modern love of nature or a native landscape. But the European aristocracy, rejected for perpetrating the First World War, were not so easily to be redeemed, even by a park. The modern movement pioneers left their hearts in a native, not aristocratic, countryside.

No one typifies this rite of passage more than Eliel Saarinen, the great Finnish architect. Saarinen was born in 1873 in a farming community of hardy northmen, proud of their sagas, their music and their landscape. Eliel painted the dark lakes reflecting trees and hills, the summer fields of corn, of his modest, well-farmed oasis between the birch-covered hills and the sea, with high-roofed houses, and orderly farmyards at Spankkova in Ingermanland. His father often had business in St Petersburg, and Eliel would go with him to spend time at the Hermitage. He enrolled as a student of painting and architecture in Helsingfors, soon deciding to seek in architecture 'a way for honest self-expression'. He rebelled against the prevailing national romanticism – 'I did all I could to get rid of the confused and academically entrenched eclecticism'. He heard the distant voices of Berlage, Sullivan, van der Velde and Wright, and gathered partnership and friendship amongst like minds. The partnership Gesellius, Lindgren and Saarinen was founded 1896, to design with inspiration from craftsmen and materials – 'we went back to the nature of the material and tried to find a simple and honest way of using this material'. Saarinen constantly undertook sketching trips in what he called his 'gentle homeland' of flowing fields and woods; he felt 'that all understanding lay in the source of things', in nature. The Finnish pavilion at the Paris exhibition of 1900 highlighted this talented company, and they decided to retreat, to work in peace at Hvittrask – on the crest of a hill above the lake of that name (now a national monument). The buildings were grounded in granite, and built of pine, with high-pitched roofs of red tiles – all in harmony with their setting of fir, birch and pine trees. There was a formal garden here, and at his Molchow-Haus near Viborg in eastern Finland. The Saarinens travelled and met such pioneers as Peter Behrens, and

Josef Olbricht in Darmstadt. Their visitors included the composer Gustav Mahler, the writer Maxim Gorki found refuge there; they had sympathies with Charles Rennie Mackintosh, Walter Gropius and Mies van der Rohe, and at the Stockholm Olympiad in 1910 they met the sculptor Carl Milles and his wife Olga.

Saarinen constantly struggled to rationalize: 'I learned that my head and heart had to be kept clear so that I could discern between the style-bound and restrained designs and, on the other hand, the debased and undesirable'.[6] Nature remained a sacred ideal, constant in all this world of change. He was drawn farther into the wider world, to city planning and eventually actually to leave Finland after winning the Chicago Tribune tower competition in 1923. The Saarinens were, perhaps surprisingly, seduced by the blandishments of America and prosperity, of being at the heart of things rather than at the periphery, and they settled in the Midwest. Saarinen was internationally celebrated and lauded with honours from the 1930s. His daughter Pipsan married the American architect Robert Swanson, his son Eero graduated from Yale School of Architecture and continued his father's practice. When Eliel Saarinen died in 1950, his ashes were returned to Hvittrask; when his wife Loja died in

Cranbrook Academy, Bloomfield Hills, Michigan. The horse chestnut allee: Le Corbusier hailed this tree's bud as a perfect lesson in foresight, accuracy, eloquence and fantasy in diversity.

Cranbrook Academy, Bloomfield Hills, Michigan. The Saarinen house and other faculty houses were designed around a series of courts set with sculptures, including over sixty works by Carl Milles.

1968 her ashes too were returned. Despite his deeply personal respect and love of nature and his homeland, Saarinen – a thoroughgoing example of a modern universal designer – devoted himself to magisterial buildings and city planning, the needs of the crowd, not the intimate details of the individual.

For those with a less well defined sense of native traditions, the universal designer par excellence was Peter Behrens, 'the hero of progressive German architecture', responsible for the design of everything from factory to sales literature, from exhibitions to his famous AEG electric kettle (1910). Three pioneers of the modern movement, Walter Gropius, Mies van der Rohe and Charles-Edouard Jeanneret (Le Corbusier), were all in Behrens's office as assistants around 1910, and from Behrens 'these three earnest young men imbibed the doctrine of the architect as universal designer'.[7] This has to be borne firmly in mind when looking for illustrations of modern theory, for often the garden is the unspoken word, but the idea is present all the same. Witness the much later discovery of a memorandum that reads like sales literature crossed with a manifesto, prepared by Gropius for AEG when he was in Behrens's office – seemingly on his own initiative.[8] This was a 'youthful

and repetitive' proposal for a company for design and manufacture of housing units 'on aesthetically consistent principles' with nearly all the parts made in a factory, from staircases to cutlery and including balconies and verandahs. Gropius stated 'the sites are to be prepared even before the houses are built... gardens also and walls and fences are to be provided in advance', all part of the unitary design. 'By means of early planting of trees and by their grouping each garden is to appear completely separate from its neighbours. Thus the public will be at once attracted by the beauty of the gardens and the unity of the whole estate'. The housing 'factory' was to have an art department whose function was to design 'types and parts, site plans and layouts for gardens and to specify materials'. Thus the garden was an integral part of the package.

A rather more esoteric but similarly universal viewpoint was expressed by Erich Mendelsohn: 'I see the site, the surface, the space; my surface, my space, of which I eagerly take possession. The architectural idea usually occurs to me spontaneously, at this very moment. I record it as a sketch. In other words, knowledge, the exact understanding of the actual preconditions, enters my subconscious mind – the plane comes to life as a ground-plan, the empty space as a spatial entity – an experience that is at once two- and three-dimensional'.[9]

Mendelsohn is one of the soundest and most sympathetic sources for modern garden theory, and his reference to the 'architectural idea' includes both the building and its garden surroundings. The discovery of the modern garden thus demands two ways of seeing inclusively – both the practical concept as in Gropius's unitary design, and spatial perception of Mendelsohn taking possession of his site. This inclusive seeing goes beyond modern architecture, and – one of the great joys of the discovery of the modern garden – into the realms of art and sculpture. The pioneer groupings of modern art and design, De Stijl, the Bauhaus, CIRCLE and others, were notable for their inclusiveness: artists, architects, sculptors, ceramicists, weavers, printmakers, typographers, fine press printers, furniture makers and metalworkers were all part of the processes of interdependent inspiration. Gardeners and garden designers were there, too, hidden in other guises: the garden was an intrinsic part of modern theory, but in general design and art historians have tended to ignore this. Monet and the Impressionists have entered the garden (see Judith Bumpus, *Impressionist Gardens*, 1990) so perhaps the abstract and moderns may be next.

For the modern garden designer to borrow from other artists demands a light-hearted suspension of disbelief, a way of seeing through the imaginative eye, and this is the passport to where the best modern gardens will be found. It is necessary to be persuaded by such as landscape architect Geoffrey Jellicoe (who spoke of the 'underworld of art') that the works of Paul Klee and Henry Moore present us with sublime shapes – 'shapes generally recognized to be as close to perfection as this planet permits', which may inspire us to imitatively luminous dealings with other materials of this earth.[10]

It follows as a consequence of these expectations of form and materials that the Froebel education and other experiences of architect Frank Lloyd Wright (1867–1959) must also be briefly introduced here, especially because of Wright's influence on Gropius, Mendelsohn and Le Corbusier via the portfolios of his project drawings and built works published by Wasmuth of Berlin in 1910 and 1911. Wright, born in obscure and quiet Wisconsin, had – as Siegfried Giedion pointed out – 'less debris to clear away than the Europeans'.[11] Apart from his brief sojourn in Europe, he had no exile to contend with either, and his 'ideas of a world made better by design' were progressively worked into his beloved native landscape.[12] These ideas were manifested by two creative interventions, or realizations, in his architectural life: the renewal of his own Froebel training as he instructed his children in their schoolroom in Oak Park in the 1890s, and his essay 'The Japanese Print: An Interpretation' of 1912.[13] Froebel's 'Gifts' – the six soft balls, three in primary colours, three in secondaries, the cube, sphere and cylinder of wood and then the proportionally divided building blocks – were gradually introduced to the children, stimulating knowledge of their 'being, quality and action', producing definite ideas, with which the forms became inseparably connected.[14] Wright was, at the same time as he was involved in the Kindergarten, struggling 'to achieve a clarity of function and simplicity of composition in his own' designs, according to Robert MacCarter: the Froebel axiom 'before ideas can be defined, perceptions must have preceded' banished his 'endless formal invention', his belief that every client must have a unique design, and substituted the inspiration for individual solutions, that the basic geometrical blocks provided.[15]

In his gardens Wright rapidly changed from Beaux-Arts beginnings to the lovely projects he drew for the

Some of Swiss educationalist Friedrich Froebel's suggested garden constructions, from Edward Wiebe's *The Paradise of Childhood*, 1896.

Garden House, with Doors

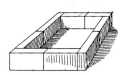

A Fountain

Closed Garden Wall

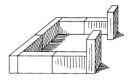

An Open Garden

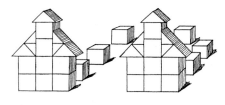

Two Garden Houses, with Rows of Trees

Ladies' Home Journal: a 'House in a Prairie Town', 1900, a 'small house with lots of room in it', where plot, terraces and balcony are frilled with flowers; and in 1906, a fireproof house on a suburban site for $5,000, a flat-roofed box, dripping with plants, set amongst flowers and trees. Undeniably, Wright's houses – epitomized by the Thomas Hardy House layered by its lakeside – assume the sophisticated guise of the Froebel construction blocks melded with nature by the application of shrubs and flowers. The Froebel 'forms of life' – sphere, cube, half cube, quarter cube, cylinder and oblong blocks – are, in fact, the forms acceptable in modern garden geometry.

After his elopement with his client's wife, Mrs Edwin Cheney, and after two years in Europe, Wright went home to gather up the fragments of his practice and start all over again, in the 'valley of the God-almighty Jones', his Welsh Dissenting maternal relative, near Spring Green, Wisconsin. He named his home Taliesin ('shining brow') for a Welsh poet, and spoke his own commandment, that 'no house should ever be put ON a hill or ON anything … it should be OF the hill, belonging to it, hill and house should live together, each the happier for the other'.[16] At Taliesin, between 1911 and 1914, writes Anne Whiston Spirn, 'Wright grouped the squares, rectangles and circles of buildings, terraces and gardens in a highly sophisticated play of blocks within a single orthogonal grid'.[17]

This is how the modern garden becomes grounded in pure geometry: in 'The Japanese Print' Wright asserted that structure was 'at the very beginning of any real knowledge of design. And at the beginning of structure lies always and everywhere geometry'.[18] The Japanese artist, he proceeded to discover, was a poetic symbolist, skilled at divining and expressing the inner nature of trees and rocks, and Wright assumed this role himself, working for the revelation of the 'life principle which shall make our social living beautiful because organically true'. He foreshadows Moholy-Nagy, Naum Gabo and the Constructivist sculptors in their search for 'that inner harmony which penetrates the outward form' – the Japanese mastery of occult symbolism, the expression of the 'hidden core of reality'.[19] It is enough to acknowledge Wright's introduction of these notions here: they will occur again, through others' minds and hands.

Wright's mastery flowers in the desert, amongst 'the spiky desert plants and angular landforms of the arid Southwest', the place that moved him most powerfully' (see chapter 3). The desert challenged Wright's architectural response and Taliesin West inspired a whole wave of building in the desert. Anne Whiston Spirn sees Wright, with 'shared roots in Transcendental philosophy and scientific agriculture' with Olmsted, Jens Jensen and Lewis Mumford, as the inspiration of landscape architects, including Kevin Lynch and Lawrence Halprin. Wright's ideas cannot but influence the modern garden, but his practice demonstrates some superhuman scale, which takes him far beyond its bounds.

My title, *The Modern Garden*, has been used before, for a *Country Life* book, published in 1936 and edited by G. C. Taylor. This was optimistic – opportunistic – publishing, a jazz *moderne* or facadist production, introduced with photographs of Oliver Hill's *Joldwynds* and Amyas Connell's *High and Over*, exuding excitement over 'taking the Blue Train' (Christopher Hussey's response to the Riviera-like gloss of the white concrete in the sun) but then asserting that 'the excessive use of concrete is to be deprecated', and so proposing traditional English borders with crazy-paving. For equivalents to F. R. S. Yorke's *The Modern House in England* (1937) and Raymond McGrath's *Twentieth-Century Houses* (1934) those interested in gardens had to wait until after the war: Peter Shepheard's *Modern Gardens* (1953) and Susan and Geoffrey Jellicoe's *Modern Private Gardens* (1968) both have biblical status, and both of them inform what follows. Elizabeth B. Kassler's *Modern Gardens and the Landscape* (1964, revised edition 1983) is another treasure. It is published by the Museum of Modern Art: the author's note in the 1984 edition does, however, acknowledge the 'Museum's tolerance of my rather unconventional view of landscape design'. The subsequent literature on the modern garden is extremely sparse, but two more recent books have enlightened my search – Dorothée Imbert's *The Modernist Garden in France* (1993) and Peter Walker and Melanie Simo's *Invisible Gardens* (1994). Some would say that the modern garden is indeed invisible, but I endeavour, in the following pages, to prove them wrong.

return to **the oracles**

It would be overly imaginative to suggest that the pioneers of modern design gave a great deal of their time to gardens: gardens do not bring in high fees nor great reputations, the chief factors that have relegated them to a subsidiary consideration. However, seeing them as they saw themselves, as universal designers, abstract artists exploring uses of form and colour, and the first settlers of the modern design for living, the great oracles can be discovered murmuring on gardens and even designing some of significance. Looking for the gardens themselves after almost three quarters of a century can be disheartening, but searching out their ideas and intentions does help to build an understanding of the designs.

This chapter will explore some of the ideas specific to garden design held by several prominent twentieth-century artists (Mondrian, Van Doesburg, Klee) and architects (Le Corbusier, Oud, Rietveld, Mendelsohn). What these 'oracles' have to say about form, colour, abstraction and dimension tells us a great deal about the development of the modern garden; their example particularly demonstrates the close integration of the other visual arts with garden design.

Naumkeag, Stockbridge, Massachusetts: the rill and stairway of the Birch Walk, designed by Fletcher Steele and completed in 1938. Steele provided powerful inspiration for the modern garden in America.

Theo Van Doesburg, *Garden Sculpture*, 1919, glazed in shades of grey, to contain red, yellow, blue and white flowers and stand on a green lawn.

De Stijl

The De Stijl movement was driven by a loose association of nine artists and architects (including Piet Mondrian, Theo Van Doesburg, J.J.P. Oud and Gerrit Rietveld). They appeared as signatories of the first manifesto which was published in *De Stijl* magazine in November 1918 under the editorship of Van Doesburg. Their radical philosophical ideas about art and nature extended into the realm of garden design. Van Doesburg (1883–1931), the Dutch painter, designer and propagandist and mainspring of *De Stijl* magazine, certainly embraced gardens, seeing them as the logical extension of his designs for interiors. In his scheme for a terrace of housing designed by Cornelis Rienks de Boer at Drachten in Friesland (1921), he proposed blocks of primary colours for the interiors, and for external doors and windows – a blue window frame, red door and bright yellow surround all applied to one small house. The colours were to be repeated in geometric planting plans for the gardens, presumably for tulips and other bulbs in spring, and for annuals such as poppies and cornflowers in summer. He wanted the red brick houses to be rendered white, but this was not done: even so, the name *papegaaienbuurt* (parrot district) was given to the neighbourhood. The colours were soon painted over and the gardens disappeared, and though the colour schemes have been restored, the gardens have not.[1]

The Drachten housing scheme included an agricultural school, where Van Doesburg employed secondary colours, violet, orange and green, for stained glass, for the interiors and for geometrically planted beds in the gardens. He also designed a garden sculpture, which functioned as a plant container, a grouping of rectangles glazed in differing shades of grey, which he imagined on a green lawn, and filled with red, yellow, blue and white flowers.[2]

Van Doesburg clearly had a real love for, and interest in, flowers – as befits the Dutch character; he referred to his 'gardening expert' friend the poet Antony Kok repeatedly for advice, though little evidence survives of this, at best, minor collaboration.[3] For the Drachten housing, Van Doesburg saw flower boxes, over doors and windows, as essentials to his scheme: these would contain the complementary colours, but the boxes themselves were painted black. In a letter to Antony Kok (9 September 1917) he explained – 'I started from the principle that all planes must be disengaged by the line of contrasting colour' – which he saw as creating essential rhythmic harmony along the row of houses.[4]

The architect J. J. P. Oud (1890–1963) was equally positive about gardens for his pioneering city housing, notably the four-storey blocks at Tussendijken, Rotterdam, built in the early 1920s (and destroyed in 1940). Oud believed that in order to live in the city, there must be a way of distancing inhabitants from the 'industriousness' that forged the pace of city life: in contrast to the street, with its severe, defensive frontages, the inner court of his blocks had balconies, flower boxes and individual gardens. For all his expertise in 'workers' housing' Oud argued that in his buildings the garden was as necessary a part of the social engineering as the small kitchens (too small to be used as living-rooms, which was thought unhealthy) and small bedrooms, which allowed adults and children, and brothers and sisters, to sleep in separate quarters. His white terrace of family housing, for the Weissenhofsiedlung exhibition at Stuttgart in 1927, reveals their row of individual gardens, for children's play and the washing line, which empowered a worldwide ideal of 'starter' homes with gardens down the twentieth century. The Weissenhofsiedlung at Stuttgart has been restored, a gallery of small works by the greatest modern architects:

Oud's family houses, nos 1–9 Pankokweg, have their well tended small gardens.[5]

Gerrit Rietveld's (1888–1964) small house for Truus Schroeder of 1924–25, built modestly on the end of a row of apartment blocks in Prins Hendriklaan, Utrecht, remains a De Stijl icon. Mrs Schroeder played a definite part in its creation and lived in the house almost without interruption until her death (aged ninety-five, in 1985). The house, with its adjustable spaces, built-in furniture and labour-saving devices, fulfilled her ideal, changing with her needs – it 'was not a fixed entity but a palimpsest on which could be inscribed a life-style and a life-view'.[6] We may wish that Mrs Schroeder had been more of a gardener (though her gardening alter ego may be seen in Mien Ruys, pp. 142–53) and that she had left images of plantings and pathlines in her small, flat, rectangular garden. However, in the search for modern theory, the Schroeder house demonstrated two important objectives – first, that the modern house is the prime but insubstantial, translucent form in its own garden (witness Rietveld's Pavilion, 1955, a transparent garden house for the Kroller-Muller Museum at Otterlo); and secondly, the modern garden is not ashamed to be seen – in fact its openness, smallness, and sense of display were an expression of community living.

Two more important modern ideas are implicit in the eager and inventive De Stijl activists – abstract ideas that have permeated all other areas of design, so it is vital that they are borne in mind with gardens. Gerrit Rietveld's plan for a music room for Piet Ketting in Utrecht (c. 1927), shows a radically diagonal placement of furniture (as distinct from the rectangular interiors of the Schroeder house) and the diagonal treatment of sites became the 'revolutionary' motif of modern gardens, especially in France. Diagonals, used in geometric blocks of primary colours, as in Van Doesburg's layout for Cine-dancing at the Aubette, Strasbourg, 1926–28, demonstrate the gardens he had in mind.

The second and larger idea, the concept of space as organized by colour and geometric form, epitomized by the work of Piet Mondrian (1872–1944) and the universality of satisfaction, of rightness, that underlies the modern garden, rose from the fertile ground of De Stijl. The rightness of details – down to the style of print, perfected by Jan Tschichold in *Die Neue Typographie* of 1928 – was introduced by De Stijl and permeates and surrounds the modern garden for over thirty years.

Mondrian's influence on colour and geometric form was implicit in Van Doesburg's De Stijl ideas on gardens, but Mondrian's work has remained an inspiration to

Daal en Berg, the Hague, 1920–21. Jan Wils's flat-roofed, low-rise estate overflows with greenery – window and balcony boxes are integral to the design. The housing was built around a central square, with a formal rectangular pool surrounded by free-standing flower boxes (recalling Van Doesburg's *Garden Sculpture*, illustrated opposite).

artists and designers to the present day. His artistic, and to some extent spiritual journeying, is relevant to the developing theory of the modern garden.

Mondrian came from a Dutch Calvinist background, and his early paintings were representational landscapes

Piet Mondrian, *Tableau I, Composition with Red, Black, Blue and Yellow*, 1921.

The Dutch landscape in spring still endorses Mondrian's vision, with blocks of primary colours in the bulbfields: primary colours and verticals conspire in this annual fantasy at the Keukenhof show garden near Lisse.

and studies of trees and flowers, such as the chrysanthemum, directly inspired by nature and his native landscape. In his late twenties he discovered theosophy, an esoteric cult devoted to spirituality, with a lack of interest, if not an actual disdain, of the physical processes of nature. Mondrian was initiated by co-founder Annie Besant in 1909, was reputed to keep a portrait of Madame Blavatsky on his wall, and his enthralment lasted through the cult's pre-war boom, especially in Holland, and until 1916 or 1917. He worked through his paintings to transform his seascapes, compositions of trees and studies of plants into abstract forms in response to the theosophic goals.

By 1920 he could explain this process in words: he proposed a view of the Dutch countryside at dusk, the details melted into a vast, flat horizon, with the moon hanging high in the sky. Such beauty stirred him, he 'was struck by the way the deep colours and tones suggested repose' – and this repose could be expressed in painting 'through the harmony of relations… For me, the plastic relation is more alive precisely when it is not enveloped in the natural, but shows itself in the flat and rectilinear. In my opinion… the natural appearance veils the expression of relations. When one wants to express definite relations plastically, one must show them with greater precision than they have in nature'. The flat line of the horizon is thus 'positively expressed' in a strong black horizontal, against the indeterminable plane of the sky – which is itself defined by the line drawn by the eye from the moon to the flat plane. 'The most perfect instance is the right angle, which expresses the relations between two extremes' – Mondrian's definition is the vertical black line 'even though such a line is not apparent in the scene… it is for us to trace it, in order to express positively the opposition to the horizontal'. These relative positions of line and plane are the essence of nature's repose, but they are inexact in their manifestation in nature: 'It is this balanced interrelation of different positions (the opposition of line and plane by means of the right angle) which expresses repose plastically'.

Mondrian emphasized the exclusion of the oblique: 'if a tree rose above the horizon, our eye would at once trace involuntarily a line going from that tree to the moon. This oblique position would oppose, but not balance, the horizontal and vertical positions of the landscape, and thus the great repose would be broken.' Both Mondrian and Paul Klee dwelt upon the fact that 'everything is constituted by relation and reciprocity… colour exists only through another colour, dimension is defined by another dimension; there is no position except by opposition to another position'.[7]

Mondrian became famously irritated by nature – his friends, who included Vasily Kandinsky, Jean Arp and Ben Nicholson (see pp. 58–59), told how he would demand to change his place at a table in order not to see the outdoor view; he preferred New York's canyon streets to Paris, because the latter had so many trees. His friends said it was his defence against an old love, his fear that the charm of nature would distract him from his rigorous artistic journeying. His probing quest for the expression of repose becomes a martyrdom on our behalf.

Le Corbusier (1887–1965) and the French Modernists

For all Le Corbusier's severe and bony visage and his radically extreme outbursts, perhaps it is surprising that his sketches and drawings of his buildings should be so full of plants and greenery. Like Mendelsohn, he saw trees, shrubs and well-planted containers as the necessary dressing for his buildings, and as the arch-idealist among universal designers, he was hardly likely to let any aspect of his projects go without attention to its design. However, immediate celebrity, the persisting images of buildings photographed while the whitewash was still wet, as on a building site, compounded by historical neglect and restoration, with new images in a wilderness, have not allowed his garden ideas to be appreciated. The twentieth century has also sought to correct, in retrospect, the essential Corbusian belief in *egalité* of design, in a vocabulary that served housing in the city as well as the rich man in his villa garden. To gardeners, nourished in the faith that a 'great garden' was a synonym for extravagance, excellence of design, horticultural achievement and acreage, the notion that a small garden could exhibit an equally high quality of design and planting was almost impossible to digest (and it has taken almost a century to do so).

Le Corbusier, therefore, must be hailed as the apostle of democratic design in the modern garden: with his brother, Pierre Jeanneret (1896–1958), he worked at his theories for city housing in the early 1920s, culminating in their exhibit at the *Exposition des Arts Décoratifs et Industriels Moderne* in Paris in 1925, which evoked both excitement and acclaim, and not a little outrage. The Paris offering was the now legendary *Pavilion de l'Esprit Nouveau*, intended as an exemplary unit for Immeuble-Villas, the Villa Apartment Block, for high-rise city living. The Pavilion was of small, private (and unseen) rooms surrounding a large living room with one wall constructed entirely of glass screens, which slid back to allow sun and air into a balcony garden. For exhibition purposes, and to shock the smart Parisians, the Pavilion was built around an existing tree, which was accommodated through a circular hole cut in the

Plan drawings of Le Corbusier's Villa Les Terrasses at Garches, near Paris: top, preliminary layout of November 1926; below, site plan of the garden as it became.

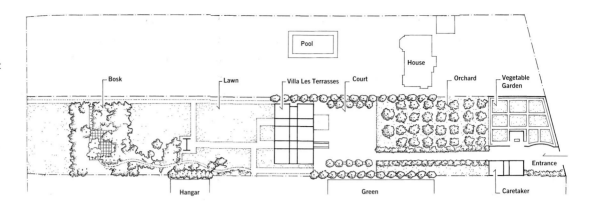

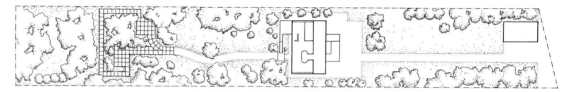

ceiling. But for the trees inside and outside, Dorothée Imbert reports, Le Corbusier's intention was that 'the *machine à habiter* would have left the exposition one evening at midnight, rolled up the Champs-Elysées, crossed the Seine and landed in the suburbs, intact, at dawn'.[8]

The Pavilion introduces two important ideas, firstly Le Corbusier's assumption that the new generations would only want passive gardening, relaxing and enjoying the view, martini in hand, tinkering occasionally with the potted and troughed plants, and secondly, that both through the open balcony rectangle, or through the smaller rectangles of the sliding panels, they would view their landscape as through a picture frame. Thus, Le Corbusier's enormous influence on modern architecture is carried into gardens: whether we like it or not, his powerful voice predicted the preoccupied and sport-mad generations who would require low-maintenance leisure gardens, as well as introducing the framing device, much illustrated in the following pages.

The Jeanneret brothers' ideas for mass housing, with 'gardens in the sky' and on the ground, reached a wider audience in Le Corbusier's book, *Vers une Architecture*, published in Paris in 1923. (The English translation, by Frederick Etchells, 1927, significantly inserted another word into the title, *Towards a New Architecture*.) In this little book, the design vocabulary is

truly that of 'Liberté, Egalité, Fraternité': Le Corbusier establishes his belief in a basic right to 'Sun-Air-Vegetation', and the new steel-framed and concrete methods of construction as a means of levelling social divisions, of allowing 'some sort of link between the rich man's house and the poor man's; and some sort of decency in the rich man's dwelling'.[9] The most innovative garden ideas are for housing estates: the 'hanging gardens' of the *Pavilion de L'Esprit Nouveau*, are layered for high-rise living, to make a real contribution to the greening of the city. They are subtly converted into individual terrace gardens, with planting troughs as an integral part of the structure, and the provision of a small roof garden, sheltered by the structure of the housing units, and with a slatted 'pergola' roof for climbing plants and semi-shade. *Vers une Architecture* also illustrates a 1925 villa at Bordeaux, complete with paved roof terrace and an enclosed garden court, as well as an extended garden with rectangular beds for flowers and vegetables, all included as part of the integral plan of the whole, for which Le Corbusier had such a famed regard.

The cycle of appreciation in architecture, especially of an unruly giant like Le Corbusier, seems to accord an almost instant fame, which endures as years and output increase, then is dropped unceremoniously into a limbo of notoriety soon after death, to await a gradual reassessment. In Le Corbusier's case, reassessment has revealed his drawings, which show that gardens, roof gardens and terraces were intended for many of his most famous villas, but that they have been obscured by circumstance or ignored by historians.[10] The plan of 13 November 1926 for Villa Les Terrasses, built on a long, thin site at Garches, on the outskirts of Paris (1927) for Michael Stein and Gabrielle de Monzie, 'was an exquisite graphic composition that weighed densities, masses and voids' according to Dorothée Imbert (whose interpretation is illustrated along with her plan of the garden as it materialized). Imbert sees the villa, placed modestly half-way along the flat site, serving 'primarily as a limit between the realm of the automobile, with its straight paths and trees planted in lines, and the loosened formality' of the more private garden at the rear – 'front and rear were balanced as if equal importance was accorded to driving and strolling'.[11] In social terms, the plan indicates the role of the chauffeur-gardener, living in the entrance lodge, close to the vegetable plots, which are screened from the house by the orchard. The drive approach allowed long contemplation of the villa: the private, leisure garden, on the south and sunny front, was a different world. Such a site, exposed to neighbours, needed careful screening, evident in the

evergreens – yews, cedar, pines, spruce, junipers, thuyas, aucubas, laurels and box plants, as well as privets and bamboos, supplied by the contractor Lucien Crepin.[12]

A drawing for the Ternisien House project – 'a fantasy which turned sour'[13] on an awkwardly small triangular site at Boulogne-sur-Seine (1925) – shows Le Corbusier's ingenuity at play in a tiny garden. He introduces the coolest geometry of white paved or gravelled paths, and grass pierced by small, square flower beds cued into the white metal pergola which links the door of the studio-house to a tiny sitting area in an angle of the perimeter wall. At the other end of the triangle he brings the street wall, which has rectangular openings, or frames, in a sweep to the rear door, to enclose a back court, which has steps to a roof terrace.

Is it to be supposed that even the super-architect, who by his very nature had turbulent relationships with many of his clients, found a modern garden an impossible dream? Or perhaps worse, a dream that was interfered with by the female side of his clientele? This painful notion was actually aired then: in October 1932 the *Architectural Review* carried a serious article entitled 'The Architectural Consequence of Women', by Basil D. Nicholson, who, though he found it 'hard to blame half

FOLLOWING PAGE:
Villa Meyer from Le Corbusier's sketchbook. Transparent sliding screens frame the view of a classical folly reflected in a pool in the park. 'From the boudoir', the architect wrote, 'you have gone up onto a roof with neither slates nor tiles, but a solarium and swimming pool with grass growing between the paving slabs. Above you is the sky. With the surrounding walls, no one could see you. In the evening you would see the stars and the sombre mass of the trees in the Folie St James… you could imagine yourself far from Paris.' FLC 31525, October 1925

Le Corbusier, drawing for proposed house and garden for Madame Ternisien at Boulogne-sur-Seine, 1925, emphasizing that detailed design extended to the plot boundaries.

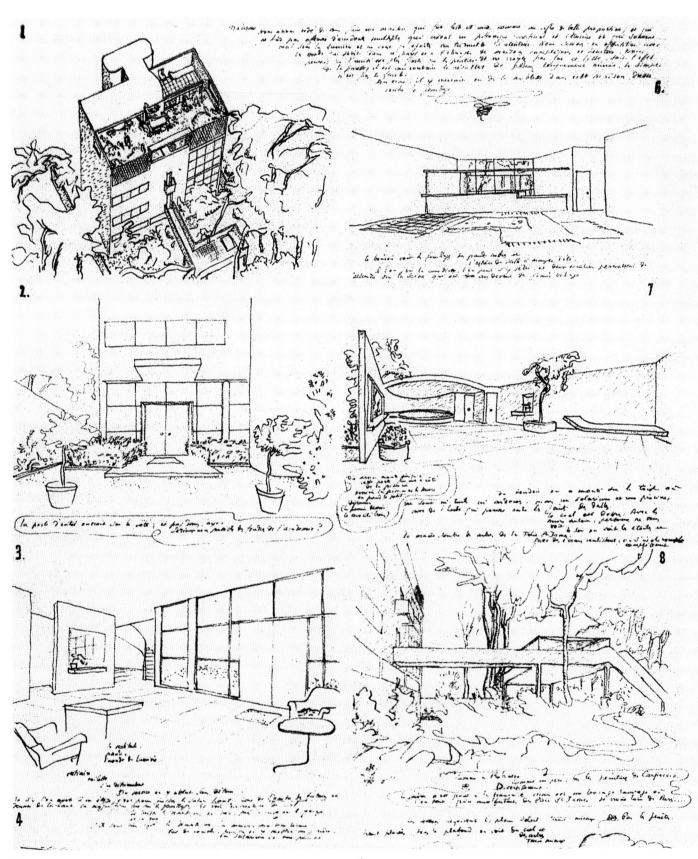

OPPOSITE
See caption on p. 21

LEFT
André and Paul Vera,
Côté-Jardin, Paris.

BELOW
André and Paul Vera, garden
for Jacques Rouché, Paris.
Both the photographs on this
page and the one on the
following page were taken
by the landscape architect
Brenda Colvin on a trip to
Paris in 1937.

the population for retrograde movements of taste', proceeded to do so on the basis of a consumer survey which had found men, in their new streamlined motors, drawing up outside 'the inconveniently latched gate of houses that embody no concept less than forty years old'. Perhaps, in Le Corbusier's case, it was also aristocrats whose ideas interfered with his own: when he came to the design for Comte Charles de Beistegui's Paris rooftop garden in 1929–30 he postulated 'three hanging gardens' carpeted with 'flowering meadows' as sky-roofed salons for sun-bathing, dining and dancing.[14] The actual outcome was a rococo stage-set of 'grass' carpeting (frequently re-turfed), electrically moveable hedges, topiary twists, a Spanish Louis XV-style fireplace and baroque furniture. Although Dorothée Imbert acknowledges the 'architectonic landscape' of the penthouse as 'a nearly perfect example of the garden as viewing platform' – with its orientations on the sights of Paris – the whole affair seemed to disintegrate into an

extravagant farce costing nearly a million francs: 'If the vegetation had withered, the expenses had flourished'. Yet Le Corbusier claimed the roof garden was 'a solution for the rooftops of Paris which I've been talking about for fifteen years' rather than the curious toy that it became.[15]

The Beistegui roof garden is not the only example of Le Corbusier's tendency to slip easily into the embrace of French tradition, into the modernist interpretations of elaborate formalism in the manner of Atelier Duchêne (Henri, 1841–1902, and Achille, 1866–1947), and the landscape architect J. C. N. Forestier (1861–30). It is, after all, easy to slip back into tradition, or to try to carry its trappings in a new direction: this was particularly so in France. But even in the hands of the sophisticates, the Vera brothers, André (1881–1971) and Paul (1882–1957) and their Cubist inspiration, and Jean-Charles Moreux (1889–1956), those trappings allowed amusement but not progress. The modern garden, it must be emphasized, depended upon a rejection of things past.

André and Paul Vera, garden at St-Germain-en-Laye. Photograph by the landscape architect Brenda Colvin, 1937.

Le Corbusier's contributions to the modern garden are most aptly summed up by a work that paradoxically has no 'garden' at all: his most famous, and most favoured villa, 'happy in its limpid clarity', the Villa Savoye (1929) at Poissy.[16] This *machine à habiter*, his 'architectonic ideal pushed to a state of purity', stands in a field, on an idyllic site open to spectacular views, and yet sheltered from the road by trees, unthreatened by neighbours or even by a Picturesque landscaped park. Here he could bring his notions of the modern garden into play, without interruptions. Thus two seemingly contradictory theories are brought into resolution: first, the *Immeuble-Villa*, the basic unit for urban living with its hanging garden (*jardin suspendu*) allowed urban man to live with plants in high-density city developments, whilst retaining his right to sun, air and vegetation. Secondly, and apparently opposed to this sun-air-vegetation ideal, is the architect's 'almost pathological anxiety' about living in contact with the ground, which Tim Benton records as 'expressed more clearly than ever before' in connection with Villa Savoye. 'Standing in a field, you cannot see very far', wrote Le Corbusier, 'What's more the soil is unhealthy, damp etc. … consequently, the real garden of the house will not be at ground level, but above it, 3.5 metres up: this will be the hanging garden whose surface is dry and healthy, and from it you will get a good view'.[17] Le Corbusier was nothing if not manipulative: perhaps it was not so much that the 'unhealthy' damp offended him, rather that a garden on the ground would clutter the pure relationship of his building to the earth. The modern architects liked the appearance of gravity defied, not only with high-rise buildings, but with the use of pilotis, as at Villa Savoye, or of a concrete rafted construction, as in Mies van der Rohe's Farnsworth House in Plano, Illinois. This was at the very core of their new technological expressionism, and they were not likely to let a mere garden shackle the otherwise deftly 'floating' buildings, which in certain lights and seasons, cleverly observed, could appear almost supernaturally sublime.

Villa Savoye, therefore, embraces its garden terraces into its sculptural interplay of spaces, and the terraces are screened from the approach. The main terrace is a sky-roofed extension of the living room, with wide-jointed square pavings, the grass growing in between, and large planting boxes, and space for dining and dancing. In Le Corbusier's parallel concept, of nature as an idyll worthy of contemplation, the very design and structure of the villa creates views, almost as benedictions on the lives of its inhabitants. The architect was so (understandably) thrilled with his villa that he proposed it as a 'universal type'. He envisaged almost anywhere in the world 'twenty houses rising from the tall grasses of an orchard where cows will continue to graze… Grass will flank the paths, nothing will be troubled, neither trees, nor flowers, nor herds. The inhabitants will… contemplate [a countryside] left intact, from their hanging garden or from the four sides of their *fenêtres en longueur*. Their domestic life will be inserted in a Virgilian dream'.[18]

Erich Mendelsohn (1887–1953)

In contrast to Le Corbusier's rather bloodless wizardry, Erich Mendelsohn is characterized by his love of plants as fellows on this living earth, as God's contribution to his architecture, and his consequent affection for his own garden. If Le Corbusier is the flat earth designer par excellence, then Mendelsohn embraces the curving, undulating site, in all its 'vegetative oneness', as the partner of his buildings.

As also with Le Corbusier, a whole book could be used to explore Mendelsohn's garden and landscape philosophies, and what follows here is necessarily the briefest sketching of some essentials. He was born on 21 March 1887 in Allenstein, then in East Prussia (now Olsztyn in Poland) and brought up in a musical, happy and united family, with five brothers, which gave him an unclouded childhood in close contact with nature. He started to study economics in his father's footsteps, but switched to architecture, at the Technische Hochschule in Berlin, and then Munich, where he took his degree in 1912. He met the young cellist Luise Maas in 1910, and they were married in 1915; he had already enlisted and after his marriage he was posted to the Russian front. Clearly he had a great deal to live for, but it was his self-belief that kept him alive: whereas it was disgust and shame that drove Gropius to modernism, with Mendelsohn it was a conviction of his personal adventure amidst the new techniques of building and the opportunities to change lives in cities which drove him – 'Only where the living purpose exists will new things be formed'.[19] He was not unscathed by the war, for in 1921 he lost the sight of one eye, which is attributed to a malignant tumour, but was quite possibly war related; his other eye was not undamaged, and he was always to wear thick glasses. This impairment was critical to his view of the world, shown in his thickly-penned sketches, his horizontality and even perhaps, his wish to reduce the 'glare' of his architecture by clothing it with plants. In a 1923 lecture on Dynamics and Function, he spoke of the 'new rhythm' seizing the world, how 'the man of the Middle Ages out of the horizontal calm of his contemplative working-day, needed the vertical cathedral in order to find his God high above' but that 'the man of our day, out of the excitement of his rapid life, can find compensation only in an unrestrained horizontality'.[20] Mendelsohn's sketches bear this out, and so does Patrick Trevor-Roper's observation that 'the movements of our eyes in the horizontal plane are "easier" than those in a vertical plane'.[21]

Throughout the 1920s Mendelsohn amassed impressive commissions: the Einstein Tower, the Schocken department stores, factories, power stations, housing; he collaborated with Richard Neutra on several occasions, he visited America and met Frank Lloyd Wright (a boost for his notion of horizontality) and, being Jewish, he forged connections with (what was then) Palestine, including the design of a garden city for Mount Carmel. Whether because of his homeland instinct, or understandable preference, his found inspiration in nature 'unspoiled, unharmed, simple, breathing deeply' in countries with a Mediterranean climate. His joy in sun and shadow, in flowers, is radiated in letters from the south of France and from Greece: 'Beyond Larissa there are broad blazes of wild mustard and poppies in the fields. The alternating yellow and red of the wild flowers recede into the distance… The Architect-Creator hides behind their colours, behind the haze of the landscape and the blue sky above'.[22] Mendelsohn's largest garden was designed for Professor Weizmann, at Reheboth, a village near Tel-Aviv, where he built the house in 1936 on a hill amongst orange groves: the design, even in plan, shows the rectangular house embracing its site by means of curving terraces of evergreens – rosemary, oleanders, myrtle, magnolias – the paths through the

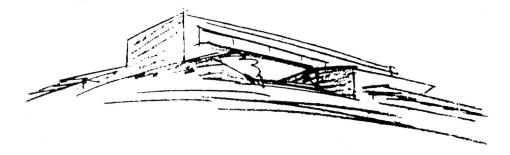

Erich Mendelsohn, sketch for his own house, 'am Rupenhorn', 1928.

Your house stands in a wonderful spot. And furthermore it does not hover, one cannot use this word: it rests! It rests, outstretched like one of those mechanical birds that cannot spread their wings for themselves. I do not know if I told you then how very much the terrace pleased me, the bare facade with the narrow corner, pierced by the windows which resemble strips of crystal. And then comes the green, the plants, mingling with the white of the facade… I can still recall distinctly how we walked through the green wood which smelled of fir trees and were all at once surprised at the edge of the wood where the hill falls away from a height of a hundred feet to the waters of the Havel below.[24] Victoria Ocampo, 1930

half-wild hillside rippling outwards with a definite force, and leading to special havens, bird sanctuaries or pools.

In 1929 the Mendelsohns moved into their own house and garden, built on a long, narrow, west-facing site overlooking the Havel lakes, 'am Rupenhorn', Berlin. The garden falls away, with the house at the top on seemingly level ground, set just 'at the point where the slope breaks away from the flat and to dramatize this fact'.[23] The drive entrance is dug out to the low-level garage, and the soil was presumably used to level off the 'front' lawn, a clean rectangle flanked by the straight paved footpath to the door, which enters on the level of the principal rooms, taking the visitor through the living room, with a view into the spacious, elegant music room with its grand piano, and out onto the wide west-facing terrace.

Once the Mendelsohns had become established, the house rested amongst flowers, summer borders along the walls, a fringe of flowers along the edge of the

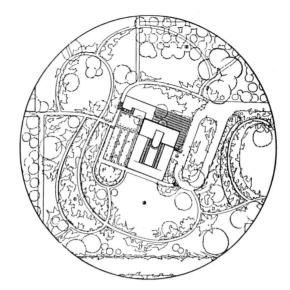

Mendelsohn, sketch plan for the Weizmann house and garden, Reheboth near Tel Aviv, 1936.

BELOW
Mendelsohn's house, 'am Rupenhorn', photographed from the east side of the sloping garden.

Mendelsohn's house, 'am Rupenhorn', site plan and detail of ground floor and terrace layout.

terrace, and drifts of shrubs and flowers alongside the steps and sloping path, which led from smooth to rough grass, and then to the pine needle floor of the wood, with spring flowers and ferns.

The Mendelsohns' beloved home and garden was the backdrop to fame and success, the centre of their lives, which brought a dazzling company of architects and musicians to the garden overlooking the Havel (Mendelsohn always worked to music, and designed his home to a Bach counterpoint). As soon as Hitler came to power, they knew that they would have to leave, and did so in March 1933, perhaps before spring came to the woodland garden; they spent some time in Holland, celebrating Henry van der Velde's seventieth birthday, and then set out for England. Leaving his beautiful home, where the house seemed to make love to its garden setting, was a tremendous loss – a dozen years would pass before Mendelsohn felt able to have a garden of his own again, and it was to be the charm of the Mediterranean sun-loving plants and flowers that won his heart.

Mendelsohn found a home in San Francisco in 1942: he wrote from Berkeley of the ideal setting 'cypresses and palms as foreground and through live oaks and magnolias the wide Bay surrounded by mountains and the *fata morgana* of towering San Francisco'. His migratory years were to come to an end in 'the most beautiful situation of a city I ever saw – the vegetation will remind me of Palestine's perennials, its cosmopolitan character tending to the renascent East Jerusalem's… looking towards a dying western world'.[25] Mendelsohn died in California on 15 September 1953.

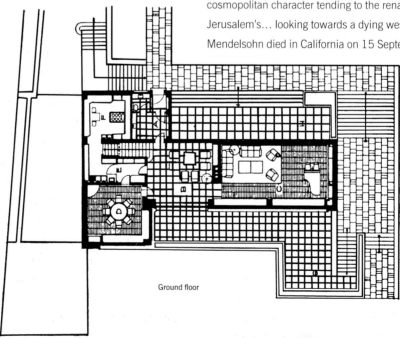

Landscape layout

Ground floor

Paul Klee, *Plan for a Garden*, 1922.

Paul Klee (1877–1940)

'Klee was an artist who delighted in the imaginative stimulus of everything he saw' – his architectural fantasies hold a special place in the affections of architects, and so his painterly contemplation *Plan for a Garden* of 1922 is a surely an inspirational blessing on the modern garden. This painting comes from his period on the faculty at the Bauhaus (1920–31). Klee used the simile of a tree to describe his creative process – having 'concerned himself with this multifarious world', and he compares

> *this sense of nature and life and the endless ramifications of its classification to the roots of the tree. It is from there that the sap rises, flowing through the artist and through his vision. He himself is like the trunk of the tree. Afflicted and moved by the force of the stream, he conveys what he has perceived… the tree-top expands in all directions and becomes visible in time and space, and the same thing happens with his work. It would never occur to anyone to demand of the tree that its top should be shaped just like its roots. Everyone knows that what is above ground cannot be just a reflection of what is below… but it is just these deviations, which are even necessitated by plastic considerations, that are every now and then not conceded to the artist. In their ardour people have even gone so far as to accuse the artist of incompetence and deliberate falsification. And yet the artist, like the trunk of the tree, is really doing nothing else than accumulate what comes up from the depths and pass it on. He neither serves nor commands; he is an intermediary… it is not the artist who is the beauty of the tree-top; beauty has merely passed through him.*[26]

Klee's works have perennial powers for the inspiration of designers, perhaps because he felt that he lived close to the heart of creation. In his work, 'as though a sufficient variety of human beings, animals, plants and landscapes did not already exist, he invents new human beings, animals, plants and landscapes, such as have never been seen before.' He presents their mutual relationships, their ever-changing surroundings and fates, their 'loveliness and abomination', and we realize that we have been granted an insight into 'the finest, subtlest mechanism of all living things.'[27]

Klee's vision anoints him as the chief spokesman for the garden at the portals of transforming art, and *Plan for a Garden* epitomizes his bewitching legacy.

fletcher **steele**

naumkeag *stockbridge,*
*massachusetts, **usa***

Fletcher Steele (1885–1971) studied landscape architecture at Harvard from from 1907 to 1909. He took an interest in French gardens, particularly those of the pioneer modernists, and kept himself informed on European developments, thoughtfully analysing them for gardens and landscapes (the first American to do so). He rejected the 'superficial novelty', but recognized 'that does not preclude the art of gardening from feeling and expressing the changes and advances that are borne in upon all artists, who in turn mould them and impress them on the world'. Steele admired 'the logical French mind' which included the Three Unities of Garden Design – 'Floor of earth or water. Walls of marble or Verdure. Roof of Sky' – which inferred three-dimensional composition, but was aware of the difficulties, the garden area being 'so great compared with the utmost practicable height of walls and verdure'. To make an expanse of sky feel like a roof 'the power of perspective [has to] force the eye to the furthest visible object'. This was disrupted by the very act of enclosing the garden, by trees 'cluttering up open volumes of air' or by inadequate handling of floor levels.[1]

He said of progressive design: 'The old axis is retained in spirit, but changed almost beyond recognition. It is shattered and its fragments moved, duplicated and bent, as is the theoretical axis of any bit of good natural scenery. Formal objects are put thus in occult rather than symmetrical balance. And in informal work, there is no hesitation in assembling divers unique natural forms such as trees, rocks and streams, according to recognized architectural principles of axis, transverse axis, symmetrical balance etc., though in a good result these methods may well be altogether hidden (but not necessarily so).'[2]

Steele concerned himself with any means 'to create beauty in space composition'. His advocacy of a thoughtful, reasoning, modern philosophy is evident at Naumkeag ('haven of peace'), where he had his own room for thirty years from 1925, ushering Mabel Choate's garden (designed for her parents by Nathan Barrett, 1886) into twentieth-century legend.[3]

He later wrote: 'The vital importance of curving from which was begun on the south lawn here at Naumkeag generated by the curve of Bear Mountain beyond and made clear in the curve cut in the woodland as a satisfactory experiment. So far as I know it was the first attempt that has ever been made to incorporate the form of background topography into foreground details in a unified design'.[4]

TOP LEFT
Curving paths on the lawn reflect the contours of Bear Mountain.

TOP RIGHT
The landings of the stairway with their railings embracing the birch-covered hill.

BOTTOM LEFT
Detail of a landing, showing the construction from plain blocks and a wall of vertical logs.

BOTTOM RIGHT
The curves projected from lawn into woodland.

ABOVE

The key to the design, Bear Mountain, seen from the garden.

LEFT

Steele's experimental transposition of the contours of the landscape onto the lawn was a dazzling introduction to the possibilities of modern art on the ground.

FOLLOWING PAGES

The Birch Walk, 1938. Steele masters three dimensions, dictating ground levels, the soaring perspective and the 'roof' of filigree blue. The stream was designed to be channelled underneath the stairway, with the water spilling out into the small white-domed pool beneath each landing.

The curves generated on the lawn are carried into the woodland, subtly naturalized into a sculpted line of hammered logs which might evoke the idea of a 'ha-ha'. 'So far as I know,' Steele wrote, 'it was the first attempt that has ever been made to incorporate the form of background topography into foreground details in a unified design.'

gabriel **guevrekian**

villa noailles *hyères, france*

Of all the garden images that came from Europe between the wars, Gabriel Guevrekian's triangular conceit of squares and zig-zags is by far the most potent, and the most persistently illustrated. Like Lubetkin's Penguin Pool at London Zoo, it is perhaps architecture that assails the realm of sculpture, but au fond it is a garden, or part of an ensemble of villa and garden. It is also a statement of patronage, of how the influential Charles de Noailles wished to give modern designers their chance to demonstrate his avant-garde tastes, on land that was part of his medieval estate at Hyères; the property is now publicly owned and conserved.

Guevrekian was born in 1900 in Constantinople, of Armenian family, and spent the first ten years of his life in Teheran; his Persian nationality has encouraged commentators to see his ideas on gardens as coming from this ancient tradition. In 1910 his family moved to Vienna, where he spent six years at the school of architecture and decorative arts, influenced by Josef Hoffman and Adolf Loos. After graduation he went to Paris, and the office of Robert Mallett-Stevens, which allowed him enthusiastic participation in a broad spectrum of projects, from experiments with reinforced concrete construction to the design of apartment interiors for a smart Parisian clientele: display work was also in vogue, and in the 1925 decorative arts exhibition he attracted much comment with his triangular garden 'of water and light'.[1] Triangular beds of begonias and ageratum framed tetrahedral constructions in coloured glass, which in turn framed triangles of mirrored glass and water, topped by a glittering spherical polyhedron, all brought to life with small fountains jetting water.

In 1927 this fantastic notion was incorporated into Mallett-Stevens's and Guevrekian's layout for the seaside villa at Hyères: a model of the revised design was exhibited at the Salon d'Automne in Paris in 1927, and the garden constructed the following year. The garden is in reality one large triangular flower box, with the internal proportions divided using the smallest square as a module. Guevrekian was never to match its celebrity and fame, a fact he must have viewed with justifiable chagrin. He loved France, his adopted home, and married a Frenchwoman, Henriette-Aimée Creed, in 1933: after short spells in Teheran and London they stayed in Paris throughout the war (though Guevrekian refused to practice) and left for America in 1948. After about ten years of teaching they returned to Europe. Guevrekian died in France in 1970.

Four views of the startling geometry of the famous garden at Villa Noailles, now restored and conserved by the town of Hyères. The planting, in essence the filling of plant boxes, is flexible and changed throughout the season, with softer foliage plants and ground covers in the triangular side beds used as a foil to vibrant tulips – or, as here, soldierly sedums, in the square boxes.

OPPOSITE
The ballroom-like expanse of the roof terrace, the sky-roofed room with views out to the sea and down to the garden, as well as across the rooftops of the old town of Hyères (left).

BELOW
The entrance front of the villa, designed by Robert Mallet-Stevens.

FOLLOWING PAGES
Ground-level perspective of the garden: the paving is of minute squares of blue mosaic; the square beds are the basic module for the design, the pathways being four in line, and the large beds in the foreground – originally planted with orange trees – measuring four squares.

LEFT

Villa Noailles was essentially
the realization of an
exhibition project, a daringly
triangular outdoor room,
set down in a larger garden
setting of olives, magnolias
and roses in the sunshine
of southern France.

FOLLOWING PAGES

Ground level is of secondary
importance, though
exploration via a modest
doorway (mainly for
maintenance from the
lowlier parts of the villa)
is allowed for the curious.
The stairs are a geometrical
joke, leading nowhere
except to a slightly
elevated view.

RIGHT

The chief intention of the
design was to be seen from
above, through the 'picture
frames' of the roof terrace:
the garden was a magical
box of visual tricks, colours
and the scents of orange
blossom, rosemary and
olive groves.

BELOW

The clear, bright light, the
bright white concrete and the
colours combine in an
illusionistic abstract effect.

britain **in the 1930s**

The auguries for the modern movement garden in Britain were not good. The general air of economic gloom and depression meant that gardens of any kind had a very low priority, except as the setting for escapism and spurious gaiety, when tables and coloured umbrellas were set out on the lawn to cheer the cocktail parties. The general shortage of work meant that all émigrés were regarded with suspicion, and this included the émigré 'oracles': Walter Gropius and Erich Mendelsohn were welcomed and supported in their short stays only through the generosity of Jack and Molly Pritchard and their Hampstead friends, who worked hard on introductions and commissions.[1] The need was for large design projects, blocks of flats and public buildings; gardens could only be incidental, and though Gropius and Maxwell Fry and Mendelsohn in partnership with Serge Chermayeff were to leave a valuable British legacy – as much by a kind of osmosis as by actual design – gardens were not a priority. Mendelsohn never really had time to discover an empathy with the English countryside and gardens. If he had done, the story of the modern garden in Britain would surely have been a longer and more triumphant tale.

St Ann's Hill, Chertsey, Surrey, 1936 38, by Raymond McGrath and Christopher Tunnard (see p. 62–63).

Gropius had already visited Leonard and Dorothy Elmhirst's growing cultural colony at Dartington Hall in Devon, and he saw the possibilities of 'a sort of English Bauhaus'. But when Leonard Elmhirst made contact in November 1934, almost immediately after Gropius had settled in England, the American William Lescaze was firmly in post and designing Dartington's modern buildings, notably High Cross House, and garden for the school's head, Bill Curry. Howe and Lescaze's High Cross House (now fully restored and the first modern house to be opened to the public in Britain) was evidence of the effect of the avant-garde upon a traditional country estate. It occupies a generous rectangular garden, beside the winding lane to the Hall, and the rigorously modern design still comes as a surprise. The architects designed the footgate and paved path to the door: on the right the paving diverts at right angles to the drive entrance, and on the left leads through a white dividing wall, to a staff door and the kitchen garden and terrace for the 'whirligig' clothes lines. This entrance and service block is painted bright blue, while the 'proper' part of the house is rendered white, with Corbusian bedroom terrace and roof garden: the terrace projects out on pilotis, over a dining terrace which gives on to a large lawn. The kitchen garden was separated from the pleasure garden by a hedge.

Gropius's idea of a design studio came to nothing, and it seems unlikely that he would have bettered the Dartington gardens, already worked on by Beatrix Farrand and to be finished by Percy Cane.[2]

If the architectural intelligentsia of Hampstead welcomed the talented émigrés, what were the members of the gardening world thinking in the early 1930s? Many must have been reading *The Studio*'s innovatory annual gardens and gardening volumes, of which the first had appeared in the winter of 1926–27, titled 'Modern Gardens', with a discursive introduction on design (though not modern design) by Percy Cane. Cane must be regarded as a lapsed modernist: he was at school with the Crittall brothers and Sir Francis Crittall, the pioneer of the standard metal window unit, gave him his first job at just the time he was developing his community of flat-roofed, white concrete houses at Silver End in Essex.[3] Cane did not stay long, preferring to cultivate a richer garden clientele (the 'Modern Gardens' editorial was probably the commercial opportunity which he grasped enthusiastically) thus missing the design opportunity for creating a modern layout and gardens at Silver End.[4] In 'Modern Gardens' Cane surveys work on the continent, with mention of Denmark, Sweden and France, but makes no mention of modernism. The volume illustrates the plan and there is a frenetic photograph of the Vera brothers' garden, the courtyard at Tony Garnier's house at Saint-Rambert, a lovely iron gate designed by Peter Behrens, and Carl Milles's garden. Otherwise the preference is for stone steps, oak pergolas and drifts of herbaceous perennials in the rather grand post-Edwardian style, the word 'modern' applied, as so often, meaning merely contemporary.

The Studio volumes were an attempt to raise the profile of garden design in Britain. The Royal Horticultural Society had staged a design exhibition in 1928 which had been almost wholly aristocratic and retrospective in content. Even the avant-garde *Architectural Review* seemed only able to use the word 'garden' when accompanied by some excursion into the Picturesque. There was every evidence of the usual British disease: when in doubt look backwards.

The Institute of Landscape Architects was formed in 1929, but most of the new professionals – who briefly included Percy Cane – preferred to cultivate rich clients for whom gardens had to be removed from reality into the comforting realms of tradition. Garden design – perhaps even more than architecture – was guilty as accused by Leslie Martin in *CIRCLE*, his single sentence falling on the page with the thud as of a York stone slab: 'The formal has created its own separate and independent world'. He scorned the lack of co-ordination – 'the separation of the formal, technical and social problems' which he said were 'unavoidably linked' with architecture.[5] This was truer still of gardens of worthwhile design, which were elevated to the status of luxuries, the playthings of the rich who could pay others to tend them, to be viewed by the rest of us for a shilling on Sunday afternoons. 'The original of this separation of form and technique', continued Martin, 'rests, of course, in the romantic outlook which sees the machine essentially as a creator of ugliness – a dehumanizing agent'.[6] The romantic outlook ruled both owners and designers of gardens, rooted in a land-owning tradition tinged with a glory that could never again be surpassed, or so everyone presumed.

Martin went on to ally himself to Naum Gabo, Ben Nicholson, László Moholy-Nagy and the other young artists, with their house rule – 'the only possible departure for artistic creation is modern life'.[7] This was

to extend to gardens, but not yet. Integrity had still to mature in garden design: the first modern movement gardens in Britain would, perhaps, have come under the heading of Leslie Martin's regretful term *moderne* or 'modernistic', along with the dance halls and amusement palaces of seaside resorts – 'yet another manifestation of that passion for "facade" which dragged out its life through the nineteenth century and which now presents itself in its most heterogeneous form'.[8]

Two architects were welcome additions to the new Institute of Landscape Architects: Oliver Hill (1887–1968) and Geoffrey Jellicoe (1900–96). Hill's first hero was Edwin Lutyens, at whose suggestion he apprenticed himself in a builder's yard, then trained as

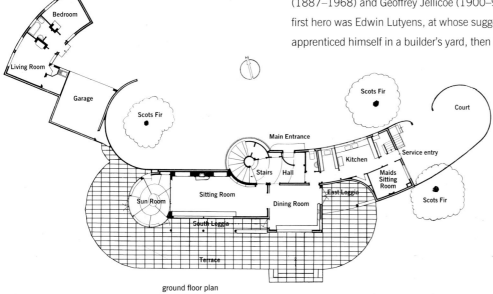

ground floor plan

Oliver Hill, layout plan for Holthanger, Wentworth Estate, Surrey (1933–35), and (below) sketch of entrance drive and front for Joldwynds, Holmbury St Mary, Surrey, 1930. Deft examples of modern British design.

an Arts and Crafts architect: then he went to war and was awarded a Military Cross. What he did and saw marked him as it did so many others – he returned to architecture armed with a mischievous facility to design in any 'style', with a determination to enjoy life and with the 'modern oracles' as his new heroes. Hill's *moderne* designs have a theatrical panache: Joldwynds, in whitened concrete tiers upon white concrete terraces, dazzles from the pages of *Country Life* (15 September 1934) as it did from its south-facing Surrey ridge at Holmbury St Mary. The design was constrained by having to use the footprint of the Philip Webb house, also called Joldwynds, that it replaced: but Hill could make terraces and walls respond to rising ground as effectively as Frank Lloyd Wright, and the soft greensand ridges were tamely responsive to his skills. Joldwynds had eight bedrooms, each with its own sunny roof terrace, and the

dining and living rooms gave onto white concrete expanses – of a lower terrace which served 'as a raft supporting the house on its ledge above the luxuriant boscage of the wild garden'.[9] At the west end of the house there was a long and spacious open loggia overlooking a long pool and matching lawn, which were set into the terrace. A swimming pool was set into the hillside a little way from the house, reached from terrace level by an ingenious white-walled and paved circular stair. Joldwynds was built for a barrister, later Lord Justice Wilfred Greene: it was a complete *moderne* ensemble, furnished by Heal & Son, Fortnum and Mason and others, with fabrics by Marion Dorn and Edinburgh Weavers, but it was a facade, with a green baize door for staff who must have lived half-underground.[10]

Hill was a gardener, a friend of Gertrude Jekyll and later Vita Sackville-West, and he ended his life happily

Pilkington Glass advertisement from *Architectural Review*, March 1936, 'a scheme for a winter garden' entirely glazed with a variety of colours of Vitrolite: a fantasy well in advance of its time.

Erich Mendelsohn and Serge
Chermayeff, Shrubswood,
Chalfont St Giles,
Buckinghamshire, 1935.

gardening at Daneway House in the Cotswolds. All
his modern designs belonged to the 1930s, when he
consistently demonstrated that a building and its garden
were an entity. His gardens had vivacious touches: he
loved a long, drifting curve, part building, part terrace or
shaped lawn, as at Holthanger (1933–35; see p. 51),
also in Surrey, and in designs for schools, with carefully
judged play areas and amusingly triangular or rhomboid
flower beds. His layout for Frinton Park Estate in Essex,
for which there is a 1934 perspective by J. D. M.
Harvey, could have been a set-piece of modern living,
had it been built as planned: the houses that do
survive, in good condition, have succumbed to
traditional gardens.

Geoffrey Jellicoe imbibed his modernism when
he was a studio master at the Architectural Association
between 1929–34 and therefore at the centre of the
excitement over the émigré arrivals. Jellicoe managed
something of a coup for the modern movement garden
in 1936 with his design for a terrace for the 'thoroughly
up-to-date' Duke and Duchess of York, who had
transformed the rather dreary Victorian gothick Royal

Lodge at Windsor by painting it white, and planting
groves of rhododendrons around. Within a few months
of the design the Duke and Duchess were themselves
transformed, into King George VI and Queen Elizabeth
(by the abdication of the Duke's rhododendron-loving
and avant-garde brother Edward VIII) but they decided
to retain Royal Lodge as their favourite country house.
The white terrace, ending in a circular stepped platform,
was built – to an enthusiastic welcome in *Country Life* for
'tying the house to its site and emphasizing the sweeping
contours in which it is set'.[11] The terrace was voted 'the
acme' of 1930s modernity – to which it had given a
royal accolade.

The wisdom of hindsight, however, infers
that Jellicoe's modern conceit was in fact his
acknowledgement of the real thing, Mendelsohn and
Chermayeff's house for R. L. Nimmo at Chalfont St Giles
in Buckinghamshire of 1935. The Nimmo House
(Shrubswood) shows the powerful Mendelsohn aesthetic
– in direct line of succession from the Schocken store
and his own house 'am Rupenhorn' – set in an old cherry
orchard in the English countryside, en route, as it were,

to its best expression in England, the De La Warr Pavilion at Bexhill. Although his work was not attributed, Barbara Tilson has examined the workings of Mendelsohn's brief partnership with Chermayeff, which began in 1933 as a convenience to them both, and added the evidence of their former assistants Colin Crickmay and Geoffrey Bazeley: Chermayeff was younger, an interior designer and only recently admitted as Fellow of the Royal Institute of British Architects – Mendelsohn, 'the experienced architect, with no false modesty about his own genius, arrived in 1933 to find Chermayeff had just obtained the Nimmo house commission and effectively, took it over… the house as built was designed by him.'[12] Mendelsohn's genius is unmistakeable here: ocean liner comparisons are equally characteristic, the long rectangular house with elegant bands of windows, a square projection which drops to the garden like a chalk-cliff anchoring the elongated walled terrace, or hull, into the static mounds of green ground. It was set high on the site – the blowing trees might conjure an impression of movement against a blue sky – to command views to the east over open country and to woodlands on the west. The sitting terrace faces almost due south, with the semi-circular landing and steps down to the lawn on the highest ground. The land falls away to the north-east, though the line of the terrace remains strictly horizontal, so that the wall conceals the garage and parking area from the garden. This undaunted horizontality at the top of the wall is reminiscent of the partners' Cohen house in Old Church Street, Chelsea, London, anchored to the street by horizontal bands. The genius is that in the country, in a garden, the base level is moulded by the free form of the land.

The sculptural presence of the Nimmo house is Mendelsohn's great gift to garden designers. He expected 'the good green Lord' to clothe his buildings, and there is an unexpectedness in the notion of a planting scheme for an ocean liner in a sea of green. It is the observer in the garden, moving amongst the plants, who gains the impression of the liner under way.

But there is a more serious aesthetic point: Mendelsohn designed with acknowledgement of a basic notion – that we exist on a spherical planet. His sketches seem to be draped around the curvature of the earth, as if the buildings might span Africa with ease. When they are brought down to human size they have an intense vigour, and when fixed to even the smallest garden plot – settling to the land form – the power remains. The Nimmo house was where architecture – and garden design in this case – became a sculptural art.

Though it does not strictly belong in a book on gardens, the De La Warr Pavilion at Bexhill must have a mention here, for it offers, in and around a public building, and still with a very relevant human scale, the same sculptural experience. Mendelsohn and Chermayeff won £150 in February 1934 for their successful competition design, which was subjected to protests and a Public Inquiry before building started in early 1935 and the Pavilion was opened on 12 December by the Duke and Duchess of York – 'by far the most civilizing thing that has been done on the South Coast since the days of Regency'.[13] Though it was immediately popular with the seaside crowds, the Pavilion was never to be completed, the adjoining cinema and hotel never built nor the planting carried out. This must have been partly because of Mendelsohn's increasing commitments in Israel: imagine the Nimmo house or the De La Warr pavilion behind his words, written in the summer of 1936: 'The house itself is still a naked babe without the frills and ruching of greenery… in its first rough coat of plaster it is waiting with robust expectation for trees, shrubs and flowers to break its angles and enfold its hard edges in their soft arms'. The following year he was working on the Haifa hospital – 'I have in two days settled a great amount of work – most important, the plan of the garden… I have juggled with begonias, cypresses, jacarandas and *Poinciana regis* until the plan was filled. A very concentrated task until buildings, roads and trees yield a unity'.[14] He could not comprehend his buildings 'without my dreams of nature' – and it is a profound sadness that he never had the time or perhaps the budget to clothe the nakedness of his English buildings. So, experience the De La Warr Pavilion as sculpture in its tarnished setting, squint and skew your vision, crouch and shut one eye, and imagine it evolving and revolving through wind-carved pines and beckoning from masses of evergreens. One conclusion is absolutely certain, Mendelsohn has banished the axial view, the formal way of looking, vanquished that independent world forever.

Bentley Wood (1934–38)

With Mendelsohn increasingly busy in Israel, Chermayeff had built himself a house in the country – entirely as his own architect and with the garden designed by a young landscape architect, Christopher Tunnard. The site occupied a soft and secluded eminence in the heart of the Downs at Framfield in Sussex, and the proposal to build a flat-roofed modern house – which commanded rolling views and thus could equally be seen from afar – caused a great furore with Uckfield Rural District Council, so that the building of Chermayeff's country

retreat has become known as the Battle of Bentley Wood.[15] The garden has a sadder and sorrier history: despite the downland setting, the garden is fairly level, and a matter of plan rather than three-dimensional experience. The house appears as a two-storeyed rectangular box of six bays, of a lightweight wood structure, with the ground-floor bays entirely of glass. It looks southwards, across a level paved terrace, with the paviours diminishing in size to create false perspective, which halts at the lawn edge but for a raised catwalk, two paviours wide, some two feet high, which continues to a given point, ending in a platform, a plinth and a short flight of steps returning down to lawn level. The 'given point' is a mature tree, just beyond which is a five-bayed 'window frame' – which has some geometrical relationship to the bays of the house – controlling the distant view. This rather witty layout of an essentially

Erich Mendelsohn and Serge Chermayeff, the De La Warr Pavilion, Bexhill-on-Sea, Sussex, 1935. Although unfinished, it is possible to imagine how Mendelsohn intended his building to be set.

Serge Chermayeff and
Christopher Tunnard,
Bentley Wood, Halland,
Sussex, 1935–38.
Chermayeff's sketch for
his own house explores
the relationship between
the house and garden.

BELOW
Bentley Wood's garden was
mostly natural, carefully
contrived by Tunnard to
'leak' into wild garden
and woodland.

long thinnish garden (the garden 'leaks' into wild garden and woodland on the west side of the house) had a further purpose. Chermayeff, probably encouraged by Tunnard, asked Henry Moore for one of his sculptures for the garden site, for which £300 was the agreed fee, and a £50 deposit paid. Moore, then much preoccupied with reclining figures (and having recently saved a woman from drowning), carved his *Recumbent Figure*, fifty-five inches long in Hornton stone: she was delivered to the garden in September 1938. Moore had examined the site carefully, he felt he had to work in sympathy with the predominant horizontals of the landscape and he felt his figure 'to be a kind of focal point for all the horizontals'. While he was working he 'became aware of the necessity of giving outdoor sculpture a far-seeing gaze. My figure looked out across a great sweep of the Downs, and her

gaze gathered in the horizon… The sculpture', he recalled, 'had its own identity and did not need to be on Chermayeff's terrace, but so to speak enjoyed being there… a mediator between a modern house and ageless land'.[16]

Unfortunately the enjoyment was brief: soon Chermayeff was to leave for America, the house was to be sold, and Chermayeff asked Moore to take his figure back. The *Recumbent Figure* herself was bought for the Tate Gallery but sent to the New York World's Fair of 1939, where she remained until after the war. That fragile moment of equality, of designer and sculptor contributing to the garden together, was shattered. No work of Moore's was to enjoy simply 'being there' in a garden of matching merit, until the 1950s in faraway Indiana (see p. 102).

Bentley Wood, the view from the terrace to the framed landscape, with Henry Moore's *Recumbent Figure* (1938) – 'a mediator between a modern house and ageless land'.

Constructive art and the modern garden

'Constructive ideas in general are not rare in the history of ideas… they always appear on the borderline of two consecutive epochs at the moment when the human spirit, having destroyed the old, demands the creation and assertion of the new.'[17] Naum Gabo, 1936

The influence of Picasso, Mondrian and Klee floated into 1930s Britain and inspired an alliance of painters, sculptors and designers whose beliefs were to form the major British contribution to the theory of the modern garden. Through a number of evolving groups and exhibits, culminating in the 'Abstract and Concrete' exhibition at the Reid and Lefevre gallery in London in 1936, and the publication of *CIRCLE* the following year, the constructive artists (Gabo disowned the term 'constructivists' as an invention of the critics) persuaded the also-ran reputation of British art 'into a position at the forefront of the modern movement'.[18] The chief among them (for present purposes) – Henry Moore, Ben Nicholson, Barbara Hepworth, and Paul and John Nash – were all deeply rooted in their own special places or landscapes, and they each had one foot, metaphorically and often in reality, in a garden. Simply by association they raised the sights of the modern garden, as they struggled for their own arts: through their work they revealed new perceptions of scale and form, 'the chosen perfected form' of Barbara Hepworth's striving, they demonstrated the inherent qualities of materials, and – in John Nash's case especially – the essential characteristics of plants. They were all 'outdoor' artists – 'Sculpture is an art of the open air', said Henry Moore, and he would have rather had his work set in a garden or the landscape 'than in, or on, the most beautiful building I know'.[19] Their materials – clay, wood, rock, water-colours and oils, were the same materials that the garden-maker uses – soil, wood, rocks, water and plants.

'Constructive' was principally thought of as a more positive term than 'abstract' and the constructive artists included architects and sculptors, like Moholy-Nagy and Gabo, who made modular constructions; Moore and

Hepworth 'made' stringed forms; and it was hard to judge whether Lubetkin's Penguin Pool for London Zoo, in its pristine newness in 1934, was architecture or sculpture.

For the designers who were to influence the modern garden, however, and for almost all of those who appear in the following chapters, the British artists – Nicholson, Moore, Hepworth and the Nash brothers in particular – provided a vital inspiration. In varying degrees their works – or perhaps a single work of an individual artist – instilled a clarity, or brought vision or resolution into the designers' minds, and so lifted the modern garden above the mere repetition of motifs to the realm of a creative space. If, as Barbara Hepworth wrote in *CIRCLE*, 'ideas are born through a perfect balance of our conscious and unconscious life and they are realized through this same fusion and equilibrium' then her art accompanied the pilgrim-designer on the journey to a particular resolution.[20]

Ben Nicholson (1894–1982) is the mercurial and unsaintly patron of the inspiration. Nicholson's abstracts summon up 'the essential nature', '[its] light, space, stoniness or blueness',[21] perhaps, and compress this nature into the form and colour of a work: the viewer's mind tingles with wordless recognition, and limitless paths of opportunity are opened. Nicholson was the magician whose spells cannot be described: he 'was much more likely to talk about his pictures in terms of tennis, jazz or ping-pong than in terms of how they were done or what they meant' and he would not talk in front of one of his works, for that would confuse the airways.[22] He had an alternative agenda which Herbert Read defined in 1935: 'Ben Nicholson who, like all the great artists of the past, is something of a mystic, believes that there is a reality underlying appearances, and that it is his business, by giving material form to his intuition of it, to express the essential nature of this reality. He does not draw that reality out of a vacuum, but out of a mind attuned to the specific forms of nature'.[23]

Nicholson enjoyed telling of Mondrian's visit to his Hampstead studio, and how he noticed that the leaves of a chestnut tree were just visible through the skylight and shook his head in disapproval, saying 'Too much nature, too much nature'.[24] Whereas Mondrian rejected nature, Nicholson remained dependent upon the forms and lights of the earth and sky. He made his pictures 'into physical events by treating them physically', by scratching, scraping, incising or rubbing their surfaces, a down-to-earth process which he associated with his artist mother, Mabel Pryde, and her preference for scrubbing the kitchen table, or digging the garden, rather than theorizing on art.[25] Yet he could speak lyrically:

There is no understanding pictures any more than there is understanding the song of the grasshopper or the sound of the sea. There is no end to the landscape or to the colour of the days. The imagination goes through them. In most departments of life it is the imagination that is missing.[26]

Barbara Hepworth's earliest memories were of 'moving through and over the West Riding landscape with my father in his car, the hills were sculptures; the roads defined the form'. Throughout her life, as she tells it herself, her gardens were the domestic counterpoint to the landscapes and seascapes that she regarded as sacred because they were the source of both her working materials and her imaginative strength. A garden and growing things were everyday essentials, in working summers on the Norfolk coast, in the Rhône valley, in Hampstead's 'nest of gentle artists' as Herbert Read found them in the 1930s, – her studio 'a jumble of children, rocks, sculptures, trees, importunate flowers and washing'.[27] She left for Cornwall and subsistence gardening in wartime, and settled finally in her studio and garden in St Ives, where many of her sculptures remain, with a rightness in 'being there'. For her,

Barbara Hepworth's garden at her Trewyn Studio, St Ives, Cornwall (now the Barbara Hepworth Museum). The large works that remain in this small garden prove the subjectivity of scale in modern theory.

a garden was – as it was to be for many designers, including Garret Eckbo and Sylvia Crowe – the link between her human form and her elemental materials, the median ground between ourselves and the earth we inhabit. Hepworth's relevance to the modern garden (in at least one respect) is that she courageously and wholeheartedly explored the unknown regions of scale, she exploded the hide-bound rules, and re-interpreted the relationship of objects to their given space. Once again, it is her journeying that supplies the empathy with the garden designer, in a relationship that is one to one, and has – like most of the treasures of the modern garden – to be discovered for oneself rather than received on a plate. She wrote in *CIRCLE*:

> *[But] for the imaginative idea to be fully and freely projected into stone, wood or any plastic substance, a complete sensibility to material – an understanding of its inherent quality and character – is required. There must be a perfect unity between the idea, the substance and the dimension: this unity gives scale. The idea – the imaginative concept – actually is the giving of life and vitality to material; but when we come to define these qualities we find that they have very little to do with the physical aspect of the sculpture. When we say that a great sculpture has vision, power, vitality, scale, poise, form or beauty, we are not speaking of physical attributes. Vitality is not a physical, organic attribute of sculpture – it is a spiritual inner life. Power is not man power or physical capacity – it is an inner force and energy. Form realization is not just any three-dimensional mass – it is the chosen perfected form, of perfect size and shape, for the sculptural embodiment of the idea. Vision is not sight – it is the perception of the mind. It is the discernment of the reality of life, a piercing of the superficial, a work of art its own life and purpose.* [28]

Integrity is the ground rule of the modern garden: it is implicit in all these artists' works, as expressed by Henry Moore, in his brief *CIRCLE* statement about abstract art: 'not a sedative or drug, not just the exercize of good taste, the provision of pleasant shapes and contours… not a decoration to life – but an expression of the significance of life, a stimulation to a greater effort in living'. [29] He could just as appropriately be speaking of the modern garden.

Moore's works are more usually associated with the primevally majestic, or landscape itself, but the serene composure of his reclining figure at Bentley Wood has already been seen, and his preference was expressly for his works to be in the open air. In 'The Sculptor Speaks' in the *Listener* in 1937, he reveals his mastery of scale with a characteristic lightness of manner: 'I have always paid great attention to natural forms, such as bones, shells, and pebbles, etc. Sometimes for several years running I have been to the same part of the sea-shore – but each year a new shape of pebble has caught my eye, which the year before, though it was there in hundreds, I never saw… I choose out to see with excitement only those which fit in with my existing form-interest at the time. A different thing happens if I sit down and examine a handful one by one. I may then extend my form-experience more, by giving my mind time to become conditioned to a new shape.' [30]

The essential adventure of the modern garden is to allow one's mind to 'become conditioned to a new shape'. The awe and majesty of his large works also impart an emotional force, a protectiveness and enchantment to his small sculptures – and he pays the same attention to a small work, or to a pebble, as to a gigantic figure. He describes the pebbles as 'universal shapes to which everybody is subconsciously conditioned and to which they can respond if their conscious control does not shut them off'. Moore frees our subconscious to appreciate the unexpected – 'some of the pebbles I pick up have holes right through them' – and he so often transformed that surprise into art. [31] The analogy with Moore's small works, or even the pebbles, with the modern garden, carries through this passage. The garden is the protected and enchanted miniature of the beloved earth that supplies all our needs: to the modern designer who has graduated from the abstract/constructive academy of scale, modern art presents a Pandora's box of opportunities.

Many gardeners and designers will name one or

both of the brothers Nash amongst their inspirations: Paul Nash (1889–1946) and John Nash (1893–1977) shared an idyllic childhood in which gardens and special places supported the best memories. In common with so many other moderns, this was a happiness shut off by the experience of the First World War. Paul Nash's work as a war artist gave him the widest reputation amongst all the British artists of the 1930s: he was a committed modern, using the bones of modern architecture in his paintings, notably the grid employed in 'The Soul Visiting the Mansions of the Dead', his famous illustration for the 1932 edition of Sir Thomas Browne's *Urne Buriall and the Garden of Cyrus*.[32] Paul Nash painted places 'which carried for him a particular charge', writes Christopher Neve, 'where the enormity of what had passed was still in the air like electricity':[33] he could capture the past mystery, perhaps even the passage of time, in the bleak geometry of the Dymchurch shore, the repetition of the mystical Wittenham Clumps (a childhood haunt) or 'the deep view across the autumn garden near wartime Oxford'. By association, as well as by inspiration, the modern garden gains from Paul Nash.[34]

John Nash, the definitive artist-plantsman, finds his proper place in chapter 4, for the way he influenced our perceptions of plants: from the 1920s his life and work moved constantly between painting and gardening. His interest arose from his schooldays, when he won the botany prize at Wellington having entered in order to avoid cricket. Through his illustrations for Clarence Elliott's Six Hills Nursery catalogue in 1926, and the drawings of *Poisonous Plants* (1927) and *Plants with Personality* (1938) John Nash brought the abstract way of seeing into the gardening world, and vice versa.

Christopher Nicholson (1904–48)

The architect Christopher (Kit) Nicholson was a decade younger than his brother, Ben, and he worked through his decorative tendencies before he arrived at a full commitment to functionalism, celebrated in his famous studio for Augustus John at Fryern Court, Hampshire (1934). Neil Bingham has noted how Kit Nicholson's drawings reveal the cross-currents between the brothers' works – the Fryern 'studio and terrace are rectangular, broken by a curve – the large window – with a spiral staircase, a three-quarter circle, biting the corner. When Nicholson drew the building in axonometric… the effect was like a Constructivist abstract in three dimensions'.[35]

Christopher Nicholson, design for a greenhouse, Kit's Close, Fawley Green, Oxfordshire, 1936. The greenhouse was built on the same modular grid as the house (see p. 62) and integrated into the garden wall. Lightly made of wood, it has not survived.

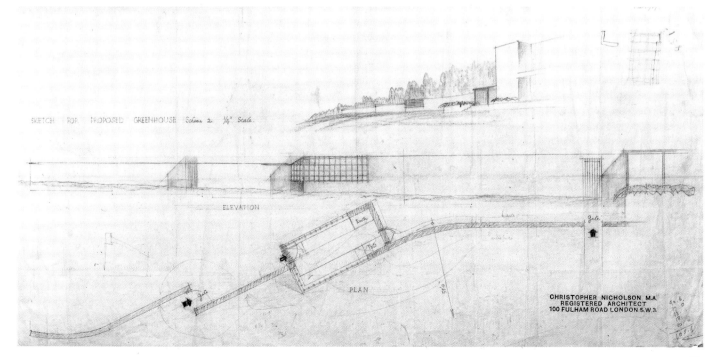

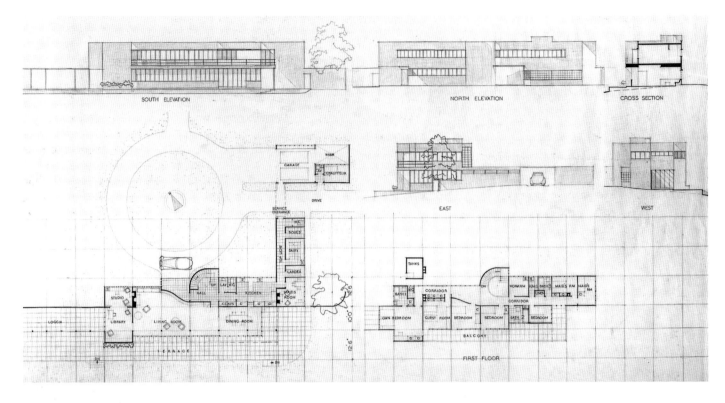

SOUTH ELEVATION   NORTH ELEVATION   CROSS SECTION

EAST   WEST

FIRST FLOOR

Christopher Nicholson, Kit's Close, 1935. The design employs a 12 foot 6 inch proportional modular grid, shown at the bottom of the drawing, which dictates the exterior as well as interior design.

Nicholson's works with the most exciting garden implications are Kit's Close for Dr Warren Crowe near Henley on Thames, and his work for the 1938 MARS Group exhibition. The plan for Kit's Close (1935) was covered with the chequerboard grid of 12 foot 6 inch squares that he used as his module (developed at Fryern) – sometimes called the 'machine aesthetic', in that it designed paving slabs, windows, doors and cupboards that all conformed to the same modular scale. 'For Nicholson it was linked to his belief in the machine as a source of enjoyment, excitement and aesthetic pleasure' – he was a passionate flyer, it was the creative force in his life (and the cause of his death in 1948).[36] Nicholson believed in factory production of standardized components as surely as Gropius did: his module makes the drawings self-explanatory – 'The rigorous abstraction of the image was considered just as important as the architecture for the group of artists and architects who published it', writes Neil Bingham of Kit's Close's appearance in *CIRCLE*.[37] The modular control was exerted over the entire creation, house and garden, and over the only modern movement greenhouse.

St Ann's Hill, Chertsey, 1936–38

St Ann's Hill, at Chertsey in Surrey is the most complete ensemble of modern house and garden in Britain, designed and built in the late 1930s by the architect Raymond McGrath and landscape architect Christopher Tunnard, for patron and stockbroker Gerald Schlesinger. It fulfils many of the tenets of modern design, of which six may be explored here:

1. *The design was dictated by the site.* Schlesinger bought a Georgian house, stables and grounds on the south-facing slope of St Ann's hill in suburban Surrey, which had been the beloved home of the maverick eighteenth-century Whig politician, Charles James Fox (who died in September 1806 at Chiswick while trying to get back there). There were splendid and mature cedars of Lebanon, perfect dark green circles when seen from the air (Schlesinger was a keen flyer) and the circle was the geometric key to the design.

2. *Mature plants were saved.* Besides the cedars, some mature rhododendrons were kept inside a woodland screen which protected the whole house site. The old house was clothed in an ancient purple wisteria

and a large *Magnolia grandiflora.* Whilst the house was almost entirely demolished, both wisteria and magnolia were carefully supported and protected during the building. They actually dictated the placing of the house, as they were to shelter the full height windows of the drawing room – the wisteria as a scented awning to the summer sunshine.

3. *Unity of house and garden.* It was apparent that McGrath and Tunnard worked together from the outset. The house occupies more than half of the circle of the plan, with the completion on the south front made by a curving paved terrace: the circle is given a tail, partly glass-walled garden room, partly paved garden court. The court is closed by a fragment of curving eighteenth-century wall, rendered in white on the inside, with the Georgian bricks left bare on the outer, garden side. Passing through the relic doorway one experiences two contrasting eras, from the sleek, sunny modern court, into a shady grove of old trees. Both the garden court, and the sun-terraces at rooftop level, are given a structural projecting frame of white concrete, which offer a variety of aspects of the cedars, the garden and the view.

4. *Expression of the plan.* Apart from the dominance of the geometry, the plan of both house and garden was used as decoration in the entrance hall, etched on a glass 'wall'.

5. *Modern sculpture.* The feature of the garden court was a piece by Willi Soukop in Hopton Wood stone, placed in the centre of a circular pool. The court is

Christopher Nicholson, design for the garden section of the MARS Group Exhibition, New Burlington Galleries, London 1938. The architect's passion for gliding inspired a pergola of tapering fins, tensioned wires, and a suspended plastic ceiling panel. There are concrete pavings and a raised planting trough.

MARS GROUP EXHIBITION

CHRISTOPHER NICHOLSON M.A.
REGISTERED ARCHITECT
100 FULHAM ROAD LONDON S.W.3.

St Ann's Hill (now St Ann's Court), Chertsey, Surrey. The site plan shows how the design motif of the circle was apparently inspired by the outlines of the great cedar trees seen by the client G. L. Schlesinger from his acroplane. To the east of the house, Tunnard's swimming pool curves around a gigantic rhododendron, as shown in the photograph on p. 48.

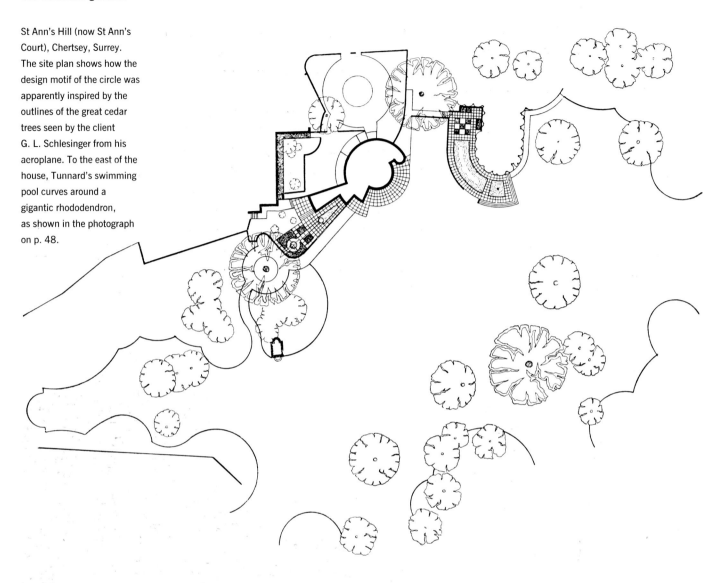

cleanly paved, with single paviours omitted for planting – a flexible , seasonal arrangement. The pools, one circular, one rectangular, are purely geometrical, but some tricks of perspective were employed, or seem to have been employed, to make the court seem longer. The pavings were square laid, with thin joints; the planters were of modern design, very like Holger Blom's Stockholm design, with some larger ones – in the manner of the time it was likely that all the pavings and perhaps planters were made in with concrete *in situ*. Manufactured pavings were used on the roof terraces.

6. *The Abstract Vision.* The wisteria on the garden facade represented the convention of soft leafery clothing a hard building. But a huge and venerable clump of

rhododendrons on the lawn, a mound of flowers in early summer, prompted the reverse of the conventional, the swimming pool curving somnolently around the skirts of the huge bush.

The only aspect of St Ann's Hill that was not perfectly modern was the hierarchical social living arrangement. The Georgian stables and yard were retained as the haunt of gardeners and perhaps the chauffeur: on the bedroom floor the main bedroom was at the centre of the circle, with a curving balcony, while the second bedroom and rooms for three maids were set apart. There was a billiard room and studio on the top terrace. Out of sight of the house, down the southward slope, the old kitchen and fruit gardens were retained, in all their traditional splendour.

Finished as it was on the eve of the outbreak of war, St Ann's Hill remains a set piece, a modern theatrical performance. It is brilliant in every way, for what is seen – but the evidence of any harsher aspects of reality is excluded from the dazzlingly white view.

Christopher Tunnard (1910–79)

Tunnard's *Gardens in the Modern Landscape* (1938) provides the finale for the 1930s in Britain. He gathered all the perceived frustrations with traditions and styles, but more importantly he gave some order and shape to the new influences. His views began as articles in the *Architectural Review* and were presented in book form in 1938, with little alteration. The Review's style of the day, a tactical mix of sleek photographs of modern buildings, brilliantly apposite pen and ink drawings by Gordon Cullen, and quirky celebrations of the Picturesque in engravings or muzzy photographs of grottoes, gave the book its character. It was as though the pill of modern design had to be sweetened with a rose arbour or two, or even more. This makes it quite difficult to disentangle Tunnard's modern ideas from his long tirade against the past, which has to be seemingly expounded before it can be rejected. It makes the book a curiosity, and (though there was a second edition in 1948) it was the only book of its kind.

St Ann's Hill, the garden court extending southwest from the house, framing views of the Lebanon cedars on the lawn. The cedars, and perhaps the palm trees, were survivors from the former house.

In the year following publication, 1939, Tunnard returned across the Atlantic. His father, born of squirish stock from the medieval village of Frampton in the Kesteven and Holland part of Lincolnshire, had gone as a young man to British Columbia in Canada, where Christopher was born and brought up. He had arrived in London in 1929, studied horticulture at Wisley and building construction at the Westminster Technical Institute.[38] For almost three years he worked in the office of the garden designer Percy Cane, but became frustrated with Cane's ambivalence towards modernism and so Tunnard left to tour Europe. He saw Swedish naturalism and modern gardens in France and Belgium, and met the Belgian designer Jean Caneel-Claes with whom he issued a manifesto of solidarity with Corbusian outrage in 1938. Tunnard had some good connections in the worlds of art and architecture – his first cousin, the painter John Tunnard, was in touch with the St Ives artists, another cousin, Viola Tunnard, was a well-known musician, and he knew Serge Chermayeff and members of the MARS Group.

Tunnard proved himself a catalyst for those aspects of 1930s cultural life that were vital to modern gardens. Having stripped landscape and garden traditions of all their mossy pretensions and excessive fantasies, he was in favour of retaining two legacies from the eighteenth century: a picture in a frame, and a prospect or view. He declared that there were three justifiable sources for modern designers: fitness for purpose (the famed functionalism), the influence of modern art, and – the influence that he felt most strongly – Japanese gardens. He envisaged designs that banish clutter, for ordinary-sized gardens, using modern materials and primary colours and introducing Japanese occult symmetry in place of 'that most snobbish form of Renaissance planning', the axial vista. His gardens would have pleased Adolf Loos – 'To find beauty in form instead of making it dependent upon ornament, is the goal to which humanity is aspiring'[39] – in line with Raymond Mortimer's interpretation from *New Interior Design* (1929) – 'Gracefulness, in things as in persons, result from an elimination of the unnecessary'.[40]

Jean Caneel-Claes, section and plan for a long, narrow garden, dominated by mature trees.

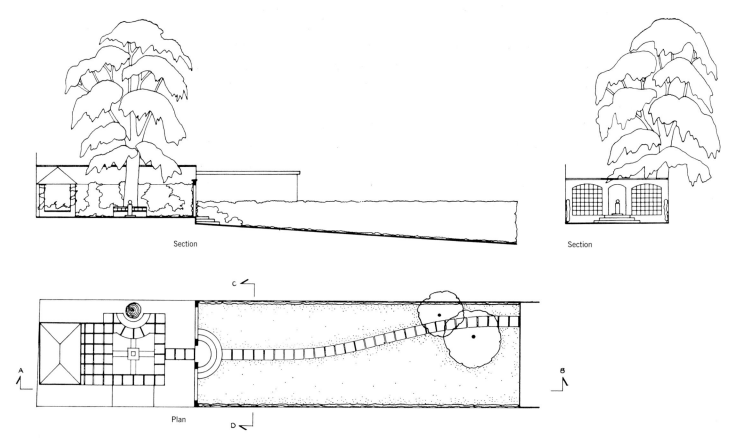

Section

Section

Plan

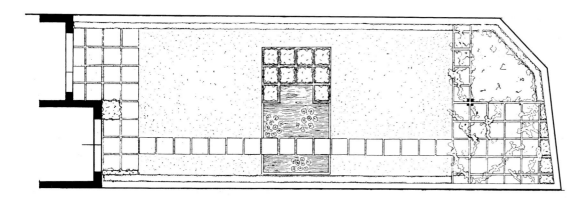

Jean Caneel-Claes, garden plan with square paviours which form the terrace and path crossing a water lily pool to a lightweight sitting arbour at the end of the garden.

Christopher Tunnard's life in England in the 1930s must have owed something to the presence of his cousin, the painter John Tunnard (1900–71) and his wife Mary 'Bob' Robertson, who had been students together at the Royal College of Art. During the 1930s John Tunnard transformed himself from a representational painter with works at the Royal Academy to an avant-garde abstract and surrealist painter, acknowledging the influences of Klee and Miró, and exhibiting with Moore and Paul Nash. John Tunnard even swept Peggy Guggenheim off her feet – she thought his works 'as musical as Kandinsky's, as delicate as Klee's, and as gay as Miró's' – and she immediately fixed him a show at her Guggenheim Jeune gallery in Cork Street in 1939. Naum Gabo and Alexander Calder were also admired by Tunnard and admiring in return.

Although he was influential in the 1930s, the Belgian Jean Caneel-Claes is little remembered now, but two of his gardens are included here. In the plan and section shown on the left, the plainly sinuous path leads from the north-facing house to the raised and enclosed garden at the south end, which has embraced a mature tree. The other plan, shown above, concentrates the interest upon the mid-way rectangle, part pool brimming with water, and part blocks of planting. The scale of the layout is based upon the two-foot-square concrete paviours, which progress without faltering across the water to the arbour at the end of the garden. Grass grows in the joints of the pavings. The arbour is a lattice of sawn, white-painted beams, supported on the side walls of the garden and a central white roughcast concrete pier: it is partly paved and partly planted.

Caneel-Claes designed variations upon the single line of grass-jointed pavings, which seem to have become progressively more widely spaced in more rural settings: two-inch joints were adjusted into curves for a ramp connecting terrace to lawn, where steps would not suit. Square or rectangular paviours could set the theme for a whole garden: with wide joints they could be planted with thymes, or mosses or suitable alpines, and extend the planted terrace or 'pavement' as a wholly acceptable modern theme.

plans **analysis**

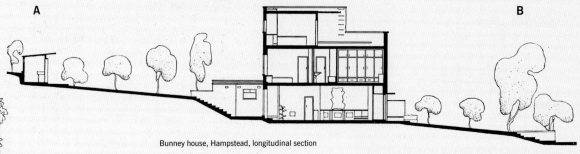

Bunney house, Hampstead, longitudinal section

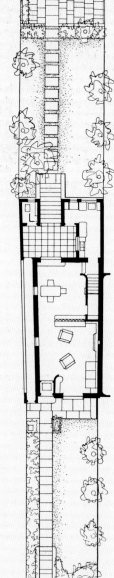

Ground floor

Few plans appear to have survived from the many modern gardens that were set out in 1930s Britain,[1] but some good examples are presented here with graphic analysis and some interpretation of their planting and the actual experience of living in the modern garden. The plans are of two types, the long, narrow town garden, the legacy of centuries of town planning in tightly-grouped communities, and the more expansive country, green-field site.[2]

The architects M. J. H. and Charlotte **Bunney** found an extremely long and narrow sloping site for their own home and office, **13 Downshire Hill, Hampstead, London**, in 1935: it was a mere 17 feet wide and 160 feet long, but unusually in an urban situation, the building line was far enough back to allow the house to be built almost in the middle of the site. Comparisons with Villa 'Les Terraces' almost immediately spring to mind: Le Corbusier and Mendelsohn had, between them, placed a blessing on the long, thin, asymmetrical and simple garden, and the Bunney garden reflects this.

The approach from the street slopes slightly, with steps and a tightly paved straight path. The house faces in an easterly direction, and in order to take the morning sun there are french windows beside the front door, giving onto a small paved terrace, edged with a flower box. The architects' studio on the top floor has a wide roof terrace, with a 6-foot-deep canopy to allow the glass doors to be opened, even on wet days, to a distant view. The back of the house has a tightly jointed paved terrace, and a flight of steps up to a loosely paved, straight path leading to a small garden pavilion, with its

own small terrace and planting. The Bunney garden epitomizes the modern setting as it appealed to a newly flourishing breed of professional couples, who wanted green and bosky surroundings of quality which naturally accorded with their tastes in a house and inside it – much of the Bunneys' furniture was designed and built specially for their home.[3]

Those with a modern taste accepted the long, narrow garden as a reality: such a basic form allowed more subtle relationships to come into play. The opportunity to build a new house was a rarity in London, and the worn-out back garden of an eighteenth-century terrace was a more likely inheritance. In 1936, when he married Susan Pares, **Geoffrey Jellicoe** moved into such a garden, a rectangle measuring 'five by fifty paces' behind **19 Grove Terrace in Highgate, London**. Over the ensuing forty years he plotted the garden's evolution, through time and growth, and the experiences of their lives - not entirely as a record, but as an anchor, keeping his feet on the ground whilst his mind soared to the imaginings of vast landscape schemes and park-scale gardens.

The first two plans show the removal of 'existing impedimenta', which included the entrance wall, a rockery and a stray building. Immediately outside the house door a plainly paved terrace was now bounded by Susan Jellicoe's flower beds, spring bulbs followed by carpets of good foliage mixed with flowers. The garden had a north-easterly orientation, so the two beds had definite sun and shade personalities. In 1936 the planting was open and varied, and it evolved through the years – as Susan Jellicoe's planting tastes developed, but the beds were eminently manageable for busy lives. The flowers made a frame for the long view of the garden, the long axial lawn given a hint of asymmetry by the existing mature ash tree: the ash cast its shade in summer but gave way to a patch of sunlight to illumine the end of the view, of a white seat against a formal 'picture frame' trellis (which concealed the working corner). The garden began with a low fringe of shrubs and trees, which eventually grew, changing the mood from an open garden to a green tunnel, the boundaries concealed. At the very end of the plot a self-sown sycamore grew to replace the ash, which had to be taken out in the late 1960s. The Jellicoes revelled in the changing moods and seasons, especially the summer months, with the illusion 'that carries humanism into the heart of nature' when it was possible to lie on the lawn and see only leaves and sky (though in the heart of London) and imagine 'a return to forest origins and the processes of nature'.[4]

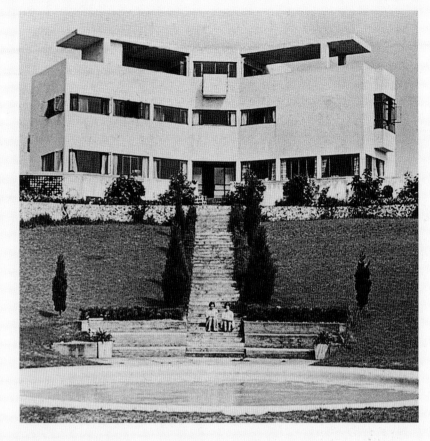

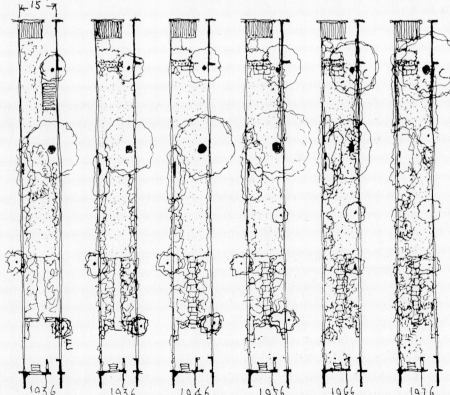

OPPOSITE
Plan and section for the Bunney garden, Hampstead, London.

ABOVE
Amyas Connell's High and Over, Amersham, Buckinghamshire (1929). The newly built house photographed from the garden side, with concrete steps down to a circular swimming pool.

LEFT
Geoffrey Jellicoe, sketch plans of his own long narrow garden in Highgate, London, over forty years, from 1936 to 1976.

Raymond McGrath and Christopher Tunnard, Land's End, Gaulby, Leicestershire, 1937–39. In the sketch (bottom) a circular pool replaces a kidney-shaped one at the front of the house.

The other extreme, the whole-hog of modern design, is typified by **Amyas Connell's High and Over** on Amersham Hill (illustrated on the previous page), designed in 1929 for Professor Bernard Ashmole. No plan survives for the house, nor does the approach garden itself, which was via a grass path of wide steps

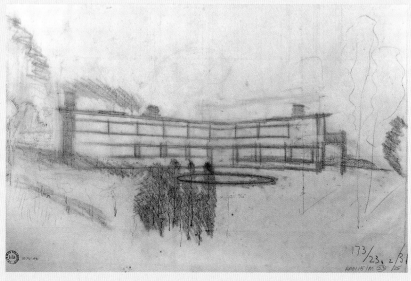

GROUND FLOOR & SITE PLAN ½" TO ONE FOOT
HOUSE AT GAULBY FOR C.R.KEENE ESQ. 173/46.

across a series of triangular terraces supported by white concrete block walling. High and Over was 'boomerang' shaped, the entrance into the angle, the 'bow' side, facing the garden, which fell away down a considerable slope: a single flight of concrete steps went down the centre of the slope to a circular swimming pool, the focus of the garden, surrounded by white paving. Grass and shrubs melted into a well-planted boundary. The pool, shimmering blue, was a brave modern statement, for a cast of mind which enjoyed all it symbolized: most British swimming pools were hidden in obscure corners or behind fences as secret vices.

Raymond McGrath's country house, **Land's End at Gaulby in Leicestershire for** C. R. (later Sir Charles) Keene, belongs to the late 1930s, and has certain similarities to High and Over. This house is also 'boomerang' shaped, close to the south-west corner of its site, with a circular plunge pool, this drawn over the first idea for a kidney-shaped pool on the tracing paper of the surviving plan. The amendment may have been by Christopher Tunnard, who designed the garden, which was featured in *Gardens in the Modern Landscape*. The north-east front of the house has a wide sweep of gravel for motor cars, approaching along the western boundary. Half the site, with the sketched rectangle, is the garden 'proper', the rectangle being a large low-hedged enclosure filled with alternate squares of paving, grass, flowers or vegetables, as time and energy allowed. Flexibility was an essential of the modern garden. On the south of the site, the semi-circular house terrace extends to a long, wide walk, bordered by flowers or shrubs, which allows a choice of approaches to the wild garden.

Two further variations on the modern country garden are illustrated: for the **Godfrey Samuel** house at Bromley of 1935, and **Mary B. Crowley**'s houses in Hertfordshire of the following year.[5] The Bromley house, for R. M. Thomas, appears to have achieved a Corbusian vision of white paths curving sinuously through dappled shade (of existing trees) and fallen leaves, lightly dressed with spring bulbs and flowering shrubs. Again, the garden is moulded to the modern lifestyle, never allowed to compromise the freedom to do other things. Much more time actually gardening would be demanded by the plan for a group of houses at Sewells Orchard, Tewin, Hertfordshire, for the Miall, Crowley and Kemp families. The orchard has dictated the conservation of major and minor trees, and the deliciously simple – and flexible – layouts for flowers and vegetables. There are direct approaches to the houses, which are spaced and set back to individual advantages, and a natural pond is retained in the lawn. The lawn itself is a freely mown space in a rough grass orchard surround, which can be managed to variable regimes, according to labour and machines available.

BELOW
(left) Three houses in a large garden at Tewin, Hertfordshire, 1936, and (right) a single house in a large natural garden at Bromley, Kent (1935).

RIGHT
Orchard House, Stoke Bishop, Bristol, photographed in 1934.

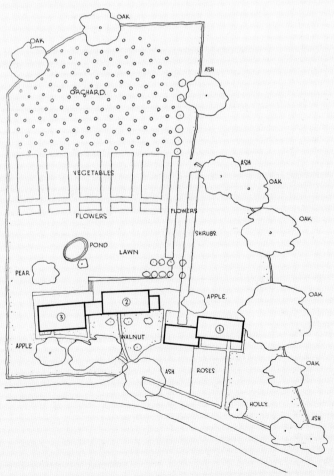

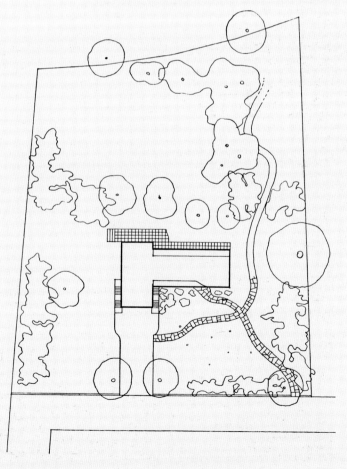

walter **gropius**

gropius house *lincoln,*
massachusetts, *usa*

Gropius's desire to live in a pine wood was fulfilled in his house at Dessau, 1925: it was symptomatic of his bitter rejection of his past, and of his search for consolation in nature and radically new design ideas.

At Lincoln the garden was of tremendous importance. The setting included trees, but was by no means woodland, and at the outset they planned and planted the garden to complement their house. After ten years Ise Gropius felt that the effect was achieved as she described:

> *The appearance of our own house has changed within ten years because the landscaping and gardens have had time to grow up to our original plan. The house is opened up to take in a part of the surrounding area and extends beyond its enclosing walls; it reaches out with 'tentacles' of trellis, low walls, and planting designed to delineate the outdoor living spaces and make them a part of the over-all composition. The large window walls are a most desirable asset... they establish the outdoor–indoor relation of our living space throughout the year. They provide a view of a natural stage on which the dramatic events of nature entertain us from morning to evening, summer and winter. There is nothing like watching a blizzard through 12-foot-wide glass panes while sitting cosily at the dining-table.*

Ise Gropius was the practical gardener – she knew every plant and 'they were always "she"'. The table from which she loved to watch the weather was in their favourite 'garden room' which projected out from the south front of the house in a rectangle, which was extended by a rectangular bed for spring and summer flowers. The living room window looked westwards to an apple orchard, with an adjustable aluminium blind to screen out the hot westering sun, and all the southerly aspects were across glades of carefully sited shrubs and trees. The whole interplay of indoors and outdoors expressed the Gropiuses view of life as 'all of a piece', the indivisibility of 'art, industry, nature, practicality, and pleasant living'.

Four views of the Gropius house. Walter and Ise Gropius had the status of resident celebrities, visited by students and faculty members from Harvard University, and the house typified modern design.

The Gropius house in its
landscape. The house was
built in 1939, funded by
Mrs James Storrow, and
designed by Gropius and
Marcel Breuer. The site
was convenient to Harvard,
to the north-west of
Cambridge.

LEFT
The public face of the
Gropius house, plain and
demure: the integrity of
house and garden meant
that space and resources
were devoted to secluded,
private pleasures rather
than public display.

FOLLOWING PAGES
The house became one with
its setting; the mature trees
and nature in general were
its projection and ornament.

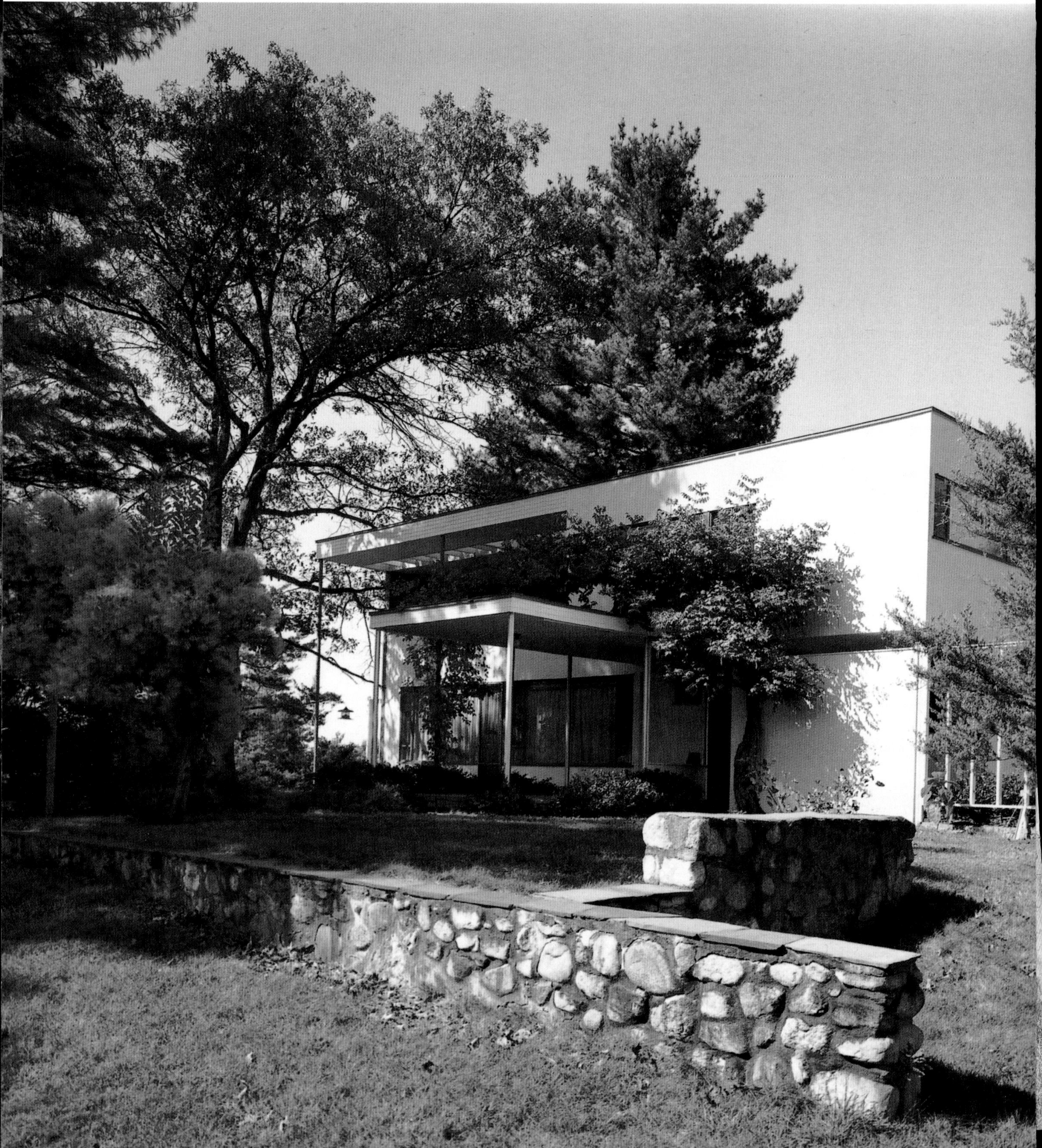

LEFT
Living spaces were carefully delineated, by both design and the garden: here the living room is screened from the entrance front. The essence of the design was the indoor–outdoor relationship, with the house projecting into its garden as part of the overall composition.

RIGHT
Walter Gropius at home, 1960. Every detail of the house, the practical modern furniture, the paintings and drawings of friends and personal belongings, expressed their view of life as 'all of a piece' and the indivisibility of nature and pleasant living.

LEFT
The house reaching out into the garden, via the glass-walled dining room which became a stage for entertaining, in the dappled shade of summer evenings, or while 'watching a blizzard … while sitting cosily at the dining room table.'

chapterthree

america

For young people today, it must be difficult to imagine the restricted atmosphere – social and every other way – that hemmed in those of us who grew up in the early 1900s. In architecture, the 'modern movement' came like a liberation, a clearing of the mind. No more copying of styles; 'think things through from scratch'; functionalism. We 'girls' at the Cambridge School of Architecture and Landscape Architecture agreed that the approach to architecture that we were learning applied to all aspects of life. We still think so. [1]

Sarah P. Harkness, founding partner

The Architects' Collaborative, 1994

The East Coast: landfall

The wisdom of hindsight now makes it clear that America was to be the spiritual home of the modern movement, but the actual transfer of ideas, ideas exploded out of old Europe by the First World War, was to be largely propelled by the Second. America had sampled the works of Gropius, Mies van der Rohe, Oud and Le Corbusier in the Modern Architecture International Exhibition at the Museum of Modern Art in

Paley Park, East 53rd Street, New York, Zion and Breen Associates for William S. Paley, 1965. A miraculously intimate modern space amongst the canyons of Manhattan.

New York in 1932, staged by the Museum's director Alfred H. Barr Jr, Henry Russell Hitchcock and the young Philip Johnson, all of whom had travelled in Europe and had brought back the exciting discoveries.[2] The Exhibition brought a good response from New York intelligensia, ever ready for the new and daring, and resulted in a trickle of white boxes, mostly built on Long Island in a light-hearted 'beach' mood for weekends and vacations.[3] A home-grown inflluence in a different social milieu was being created by the landscape architect Fletcher Steele (1875–1971) at Naumkeag in Massachusetts (see masterwork pp. 38–39). This garden became a powerful visual influence but the theories were not extended into other gardens.

In 1936 Dean Joseph Hudnut of Harvard's Graduate School of Design travelled in Britain and Europe looking for the talents who could bring the modern movement to America: he famously rejected Mies (disapproving of his marital state)[4] and wooed Walter Gropius, who duly arrived at Harvard in March 1937, to take up his academic duties in the fall (see masterwork pp. 71–80). But (a fact less commented upon) Dean Hudnut also met Christopher Tunnard and the opinions expressed in *Gardens in the Modern Landscape* were thus immediately transferred to Harvard; Tunnard himself soon followed. The New York World's Fair of that year was enthusiastically modern: Niemeyer and Costa's Brazilian pavilion had a planting scheme by Roberto Burle Marx, and the General Motors exhibit was laid out by a young landscape architect of Californian upbringing with a Harvard MLA (1938) named Garrett Eckbo (b. 1910). Eckbo and his Graduate School of Design contemporaries, James Rose and Dan Kiley, had been straining at the leash of the European traditions. 'Pictures, pictures pictures. What about environment? How about three-dimensional space experience?' These are some of the frustrated comments Eckbo had scrawled in the margins of his Harvard textbook.[5] Exposure as a designer at the World's Fair had given Eckbo's views an airing in *The Studio* 'Gardens and Gardening' volume (1939), and all three of them, Eckbo, Rose and Kiley, were making their voices heard: in the best 'manifesto' traditions of Naum Gabo and

Tunnard, these three Harvard graduates expounded their views in the architectural press in 1938 and 1939, in what amounted to a new social and design agenda for landscape architects, and their 'revolution' has largely formed the modern profession. Their commitment to modern art was confirmed by James Rose: 'The constructivists probably have the most to offer [landscape] design because their work deals with space relation in volume. The sense of transparency, and of invisibility broken by a succession of planes, as found in their constructions, if translated into terms of outdoor material, would be an approach sufficient in itself to free us from the limitations imposed by the axial system'.[6] All three understood garden scale perfectly, they took their inspiration from garden design, but their heroic courses soon led them to large-scale landscapes, where this book cannot follow.

Tunnard's reputation in the form of *Gardens in the Modern Landscape* had preceded him to America for good or ill. Dean Hudnut and Walter Gropius welcomed him to Harvard where he lectured and designed a few gardens. In 1943 he was drafted into the Royal Canadian Air Force but within two years he was back in America, this time at Yale, discharged after (like Mendelsohn) losing the sight of one eye in an accident. At Yale he was to write many very distinguished books on city planning throughout the 1950s and 1960s, and in retirement in New Haven in the 1970s he was active in historic preservation.[7] He clearly mellowed with age, leaving all his passion for modern gardens to his youth: a few gardens and a piece called 'Modern Gardens for Modern Houses,' published in *Landscape Architecture* in 1942, are his American legacy.[8]

'Modern Gardens for Modern Houses' is really *Gardens in the Modern Landscape* shorn of all the woolly European garden history that Americans clearly did not need. Tunnard (somewhat surprisingly in *Landscape Architecture* magazine) was addressing 'the man in the street' who was to seek that rare bird, a garden designer who understood both modern living and modern architecture, who would reject all the design clichés (the development of an axis, a view, with applied patterns and standard details) and concede that 'the right style for the

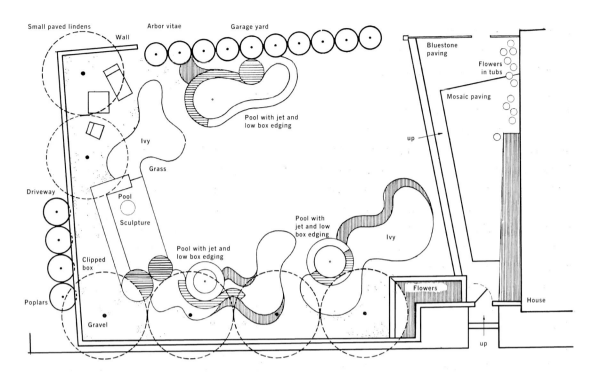

Labels on plan: Small paved lindens · Wall · Arbor vitae · Garage yard · Bluestone paving · Flowers in tubs · Mosaic paving · up · Pool with jet and low box edging · Ivy · Grass · Driveway · Pool · Sculpture · Pool with jet and low box edging · Ivy · Clipped box · Pool with jet and low box edging · Flowers · House · Poplars · Gravel · up

Christopher Tunnard, plan for a garden of flowing spaces at Newport, Rhode Island, published in the 1948 edition of *Gardens in the Modern Landscape*.

twentieth century is no style at all, but a new conception of planning the human environment'. (Tunnard's prose becomes grandiloquent when he addresses landscape planning, and here with 'human environment' we are in danger of losing the garden ground, but not just yet.) One of his best points is that space should be allowed to *flow* through the garden, in a three-dimensional way: the flow is engendered by breaking down divisions between areas of the garden, using screens, setting them at angles, and planting 'barriers' that can be seen through. This is well demonstrated in a very small and enclosed Tunnard garden for 4 Buckingham Street, Cambridge, Massachusetts, where he used angled wooden screens and 'found' objects which beckon and divert – these were inspired by the works of the painter Paul Nash, whom he had met in England.[9] Ideas and the variety of materials seem to overpower the small space: the ground surfaces were grass, white marble chippings, purple granite, concrete paving slabs and bluestone. The diagonal emphasis is thoroughly modern, highlighted by a screen: the 'objet trouvé' at the right end of the screen, on a platform (of bluestone or purple granite) is sea-worn root and another was placed on the white chipping-bed in front of the screen.

'Modern Gardens for Modern Houses' alludes to new materials for gardens, glass, weatherproofed plywood and concrete (he also mentions Wells Coates's asbestos sheeting for plant supports and asbestos moulded into plant containers). The flow of space is also illustrated in a garden at Newport, Rhode Island (above): a loosely triangular lawn spreads from the house terrace, narrowing to an angled and off-centre free-standing hedge of clipped box. In front of the hedge is a rectangular black pool with a golden bronze lacquered abstract sculpture (a chimerical font) by Jean Arp, balanced by clumps of clipped yew. The left-hand side of the lawn has two semi-circular bays of yew hedging around circular pools, these shallow for birds, with fountains, low box edgings and sinuous beds of ivies between them. The right-hand side of the lawn has a larger but similar pool with a fountain. Small-leaved limes have been planted, with the intention of pleaching them, balanced by a tight row of thuyas on the right behind the larger pool. The design of the garden is based on form, light and shade – flowing, flexible outer space that reflects the design of the interiors, with a limited use of plants for very specifically architectural purposes.[10]

Tunnard, like so many of his contemporaries, felt a need to serve society that would take him out of the garden and into city planning: space flowing within walls and fences, plants treasured for shade, ground cover, or show – all these were the private environment of the garden. Tunnard saw the modern thinking, the idea of working with nature, as the real goal: housing in the landscape means that the garden is merely the transition between the home and the shared surroundings, merely a part of a desired humanized landscape for living. He saw the freedom and flexibility that modern design brought as the key to enlightened attitudes:

(1) an aesthetic economy: 'In an ordered landscape we can surely be content with less insistent order in our private grounds… [perhaps satisfaction] in the simple arrangement of a path, a plant, a tree. Somewhere a well-cultivated plot produces flowers, fruit and all those vegetables we care to grow rather than to buy. There need no longer be any attempt at show or picturesque composition'.

(2) a new judgment of views: 'With the changed attitude to nature, which has banished fear, there need no longer be any dislike for the urban view'. All efforts to screen can be relinquished and resources put to good design and better siting. We can learn to accept most things in our view, if prejudice is swept away.

His final advice to 'those interested in modern garden planning' is not to go to a fashionable designer but: 'Go out and study the design of orchards, of truck gardens and experimental grounds… Gardening is not a fine art: it is an art of the people. In the planning of these useful areas you will discover true organization. Go out and study nature's living structures, the detail of a woodland scene, the balance held within a community of plants … Study the larger works of man to gain a sense of scale: new forms of shelter, the gigantic sculptures of the oil derricks, the simple pattern of a fish hatchery. Watch how water flows from a big dam, how steam shovels cut the mountainside in search of gravel … books, studios, dictated standards of beauty can never supplant the faculty of observation … And reality lies in the world between today and tomorrow, the realm of the modern movement in science and in art'.[11]

When the second edition of *Gardens in the Modern Landscape* was issued in 1948, Dean Joseph Hudnut's observations on 'The Modern Garden' had been appended: the significance of this was of course that he was not a designer, but an educator. Dean Hudnut picks up where Tunnard left off in 1942: he was impatient of novelty masquerading as modern design. He quoted Richard Neutra – 'the essential characteristic of the modern house is friendliness to the out-of-doors' – he gradually made the case for the view, for topography and techniques, for modern man who 'will remake nature in his own image'. After a dazzling dissertation on the 'adventure' of the modern house, of the free disposition of spaces 'lightly confined by thin contours', of rooms that throw open their walls, of surfaces clear of ornament and shadow, the delight of mechanical servants, the crystalline elegance of form and of plane, the Dean confidently found his new aesthetic. He believed this was exhibited 'in the new quality of space and in the new command of space'. He concluded, 'we did not see, until the architect threw down his walls [or made them of glass] that the space of house and that of garden are parts of a single organism: that the secret of unity lies in a unity of spatial sequences. The new vision has dissolved the ancient boundary between architecture and landscape architecture'.[12]

There was a danger that this new vision had also dissolved the modern garden: it certainly prompted an historical view that modern designers were not interested in gardens, and that, rather in the way of William Kent who 'leapt the fence to find all nature was a garden', so the landscape architects would ignore the fences and see only landscape planning and city regions. What was really happening, in those far away post-war years, was that the profession of landscape architecture had to cling to this new-found modern vision if it was to survive. Frederick Law Olmsted (1822–1903) had founded the first landscape architectural firm in 1858 (with Central Park, New York) which closed in 1945. In America, where the long dominance of Olmsted's firm and the Beaux-Arts practitioners was finally fading, the landscape schools were desperate for a purpose. In the modern movement they had found it, despite a European war. They had to grasp the opportunity: the post-war enthusiasm to create a 'brave new world' (and really mean it, this time) had to be harnessed to the reborn, enlightened profession. No mere garden would be allowed to stand in the way.

The interplay of east and west, between the twin design meccas of Harvard and Berkeley, is a constant theme in the development of the modern garden. Sixty years on it is possible to conclude that, apart from the novelty of modernism, New England traditions reasserted themselves (in a later twentieth century revival of colonial formalism softened by planting), and the true home of the modern garden was to be California.

Garrett Eckbo (b. 1910)

What we now term the California school of modern gardens was inspired by two designers, Garret Eckbo and Thomas Church, and I am inclined to give Eckbo the pride of place. He was born in Cooperstown, New York, in 1910, of an American mother and Norwegian father, who parted when he was four: mother and son left for Alameda on the eastern shore of San Francisco Bay, where he grew up, consciously 'a poor boy in an affluent community'.[13] Six months spent in Oslo with a lawyer uncle and his family when he was nineteen gave him a new perspective on nature, and when he returned

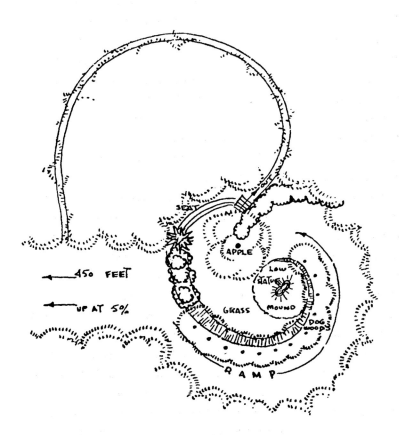

TREATMENT OF AN OPENING AT THE END OF A FOUR HUNDRED AND FIFTY FOOT AL LEE' CUT THRU DENSE NATURAL WOODS – DEVELOPED AS AN ABSTRACT COMPOSITION IN PLASTIC FORM. RAMPED EARTH PLANES MEET AT A LOW MOUND, FROM WHICH RISES A PIECE OF MODERN SCULPTURE WHOSE SMOOTH FORMS BLEND READILY WITH THE EARTH FORMS. LINKED DOGWOOD TREES AND A GNARLED APPLE PLAY THEIR PART IN A THREE-DIMENSIONAL COMPOSITION. SIMPLE NATURAL MATERIALS, COMBINED IN A SCULPTURAL MANNER.

450 FEET
UP AT 5%
SEAT
APPLE
LOW NATURAL MOUND
GRASS
DOGWOODS
RAMP

Sketch by Garrett Eckbo for *The Studio*'s 'Gardens and Gardening' annual, 1939.

to America in the gloom of the 1929 Wall Street Crash, he went to Berkeley to study landscape architecture, a full immersion in Beaux-Arts tradition. For a year he worked in a Pomona Valley nursery, designing gardens and learning thoroughly about what would and would not grow in California. He won a scholarship to Harvard, arriving in September 1936 – to be, with James Rose and Dan Kiley, just in time to ride the 'rebellion'. Eckbo, a small, tough, athletic powerhouse of a person, was already a fairly angry young man; finding the Graduate School of Design teaching droned on in its seemingly endless promotion of the primacy of the eighteenth-century English landscape style, he exploded in fury at the endless, futile shifts of fashion, all so long ago. The margin notes in his textbook are telling: 'Why must we be naturalistic *or* formal? What about the gradations in between? The fallacious nature vs. man concept… Isn't it time to put man and nature back together again?'[14]

Gropius and Breuer had arrived at Harvard in 1937, and Eckbo had almost certainly acquired a copy of *CIRCLE* and Constructivist literature, and then Tunnard's *Architectural Review* articles the following year. This meant that by the time Eckbo was back in California (he graduated in 1938) he was well on the way to finding the answers to his questions, and coming to his own needful, symbiotic understanding of modern design. Towards the end of 1938 he was, he recalled 'probably becoming conscious of Thomas Church's garden design innovations in the Bay Area' but his own convictions were rock solid, and he wanted an agenda with a social tinge. He wrote an article, 'Gardens in the City', advocating alternative designs for a hypothetical block of typical San Francisco row houses, including such phrases as 'Gardens are places in which people live out of doors' … 'Design shall be three-dimensional. People live in volumes, not planes', … 'Design shall be areal [sic] not axial' … 'Design shall be dynamic, not static'.[15] Especially in the latter mood, Eckbo was developing a drawing style which was dynamic, with trees depicted as waving shapes as if in the breeze rather than as static circles, and the use of axonometrics to give a feeling of space.

The most forceful exposition of his ideas was in an article published in *The Studio* in 1939: here Eckbo recognized the basic and primary problem of the garden as the integration of the carefully ordered geometry of architecture with the apparent disorder, or at least fluid and organic form, of the natural site. The answer was not the imposition of either extreme upon the other, but an intimate blending of the two: the mere act of planting an ivy or ceanothus softens the geometry and the careful placing of designed elements in elevation in the garden suggests order. His most characteristic stroke was on the subject of 'space' – a garden in which the majority of the interest lies below the plane of the normal eye level fails, 'man needs things around him and over him, as well as underfoot, to feel that sense of security and seclusion so essential to a good garden'. This was to be one of the major lessons of the California school, where people needed not merely 'things' around them, but shade for both people and plants became a design necessity.[16]

Eckbo's appreciation of 'space', the three-dimensional experience (drawing a garden as a roofless box), allied him to artists and sculptors, especially Constructivists, with whom he felt such sympathy: he extends this into belief in the 'ultimate aesthetic possibilities' of materials. For the garden, he names the four fundamentals, earth, plants, rocks and water – 'The technique of earthwork is engineering but its concept of form should be completely sculptural, a three dimensional modelling … to produce the most expressive form without catering to naturalistic or historic precedent. Planting is an arrangement of individual units of infinite variety in form, colour and texture: groupings organize space and make three-dimensional compositions akin to those produced by paintings and sculpture. (Cultural requirements should be so absorbed as to be automatic and "irrelevant" associations with botany, horticulture or nature worship would be eliminated.) Rocks are three-dimensional forms, the fundamental objects, and water is their complementary plastic and expressive element. All other materials must be subordinated to these four primary materials or the organic integration of man with nature is lost.'[17] Above all the garden was the connecting point between man and nature.

By his own estimation, he had designed close to 1,100 gardens: he was unfit for military service because of an injury sustained in a car accident and he worked for the Farm Security Administration designing work camps during the war.[18] In 1945 his famous landscape firm, with Edward A Williams and Robert Royston, got into its influential stride. Eckbo's first book, *Landscape for Living*, was published in 1950, and he continued writing, drawing, designing and teaching to become the idol of post-war generations of landscape students all over the world. Though he has been firmly drafted into the ranks of crusaders for landscape architecture, Eckbo has never forgotten that to reach the socially desirable designed landscape or city region, we invariably have to cross a garden.

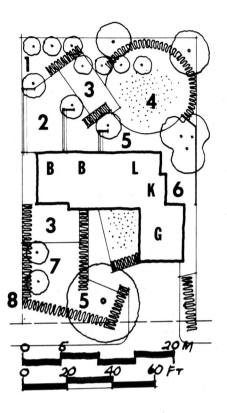

Modern garden design
by Garrett Eckbo, 1945.
KEY:
1 Play area
2 Children's yard
3 Flower area
4 Grass
5 Decomposed granite
6 Service yard
7 Fruit trees
8 Shrub hedges
B Bedroom
L Living room
K Kitchen
G Garage

'While the individual garden remains the ancestor of most landscape design, and while it will continue to be an important source of individual recreation, the fact remains that most urbanites do not nor cannot have access to one. And even when (or if) each dwelling unit has its private garden, the most important aspects of an urban recreational environment will lie outside its boundaries. The recreation of the city, like its work and its life, remains essentially a social problem'.[19]

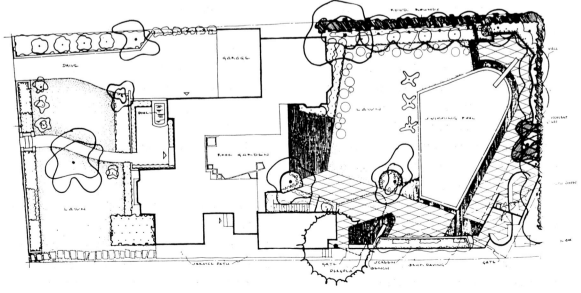

Garrett Eckbo, pool garden, Beverly Hills, California: drawing a garden as a box of visual tricks to convey visual experience.

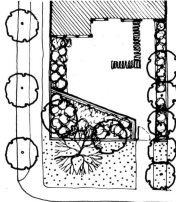

were carefully cut to accommodate the Californian live-oaks growing there: their trunks, quirky and irregular, casting long shadows, were transformed into abstract sculptures. Church had a long-remembered meeting with Fletcher Steele in the 1920s, and quoted Steele's advice 'to take the wall around the tree', knowing that the tree is more important than any design rule.[23]

A second justly famous garden by Church, contemporary with the Donnell but much smaller, is the beach house at Aptos, south of San Francisco, where the redwood decking, with zig-zag emphasis reminiscent of De Stijl geometrics, serves a similar dual purpose, protecting the sand dunes and allowing the sand to be swept through (returned to the dune) rather than enter the house.

OPPOSITE TOP
Thomas Church, two small garden plans.

OPPOSITE BELOW
Thomas Church, the Donnell garden, Sonoma, California, 1948. Raised beds of cedarwood give deep and cool soil for herbs and salads.

LEFT
The Donnell garden, Sonoma, California.

BELOW
The Aptos garden, California.

Privacy

Scale induction

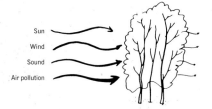

Filter and diffuser

Mystery

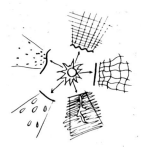

Transmitter (cast shadow pattern)

Wind control

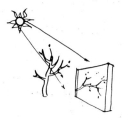

Receiver (shadow plane)

Decorative surface

Proper background

Background should not
compete in interest

Sun control

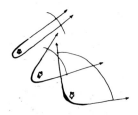

Visual control

THIS PAGE
The vocabulary of spatial
design, sketches from
J. O. Simonds's *Landscape
Architecture*, 1961.
A design language developed
in American landscape
offices, but it was equally
valid for the modern garden.

OPPOSITE
The garden as a box
of sensual tricks:

TOP
Informality organized into
formal shapes. Drawing
by Lawrence Halprin, to
illustrate the 'contemporary'
garden in Sylvia Crowe's
Garden Design, 1958.

CENTRE AND BOTTOM RIGHT
Section and plan for Thomas
Church's Kirkham garden,
San Francisco, 1948, drawn
by Lawrence Halprin.

BOTTOM LEFT
The Naify garden, Woodside,
California, axonometric
presentation by Robert
Royston of Eckbo, Royston
and Williams.

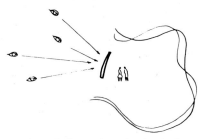

Enclosure may be light to solid

An arc of enframement may give adequate privacy

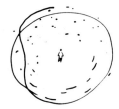

Enclosure by dispersed plan elements

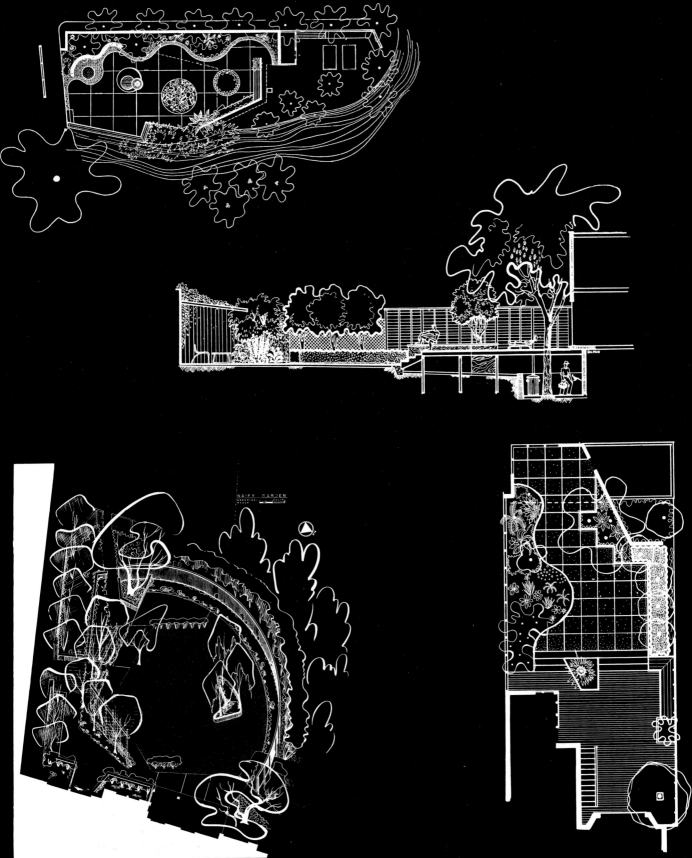

NAIFY GARDEN

Thomas Church lived and practised in San Francisco into a distinguished and celebrated old age; he was regarded as the doyen of American garden design. His autobiography was published in 1955, and its title *Gardens are for People* is very telling: his clients were of supreme importance. Recognizing that not all of them wanted a modern garden, Church never lost his facility at returning to axial planning. Above all, it was they who made it possible for him to be content and happy working on gardens, rather than landscape design.

The modern garden flourished in California, and especially the Bay Area around San Francisco, in the late 1940s and the 1950s as never before; the most optimistic moments of the 1930s in Britain were reborn with extra vigour. Church's success at transforming city and suburban lots gave him influence with the well-established *Sunset* Magazines, resulting in a wide coverage of a high standard of designs, with credit given to the designers, who – at least in the early days – invariably worked in Church's or Eckbo's office. *Sunset* adopted much of Eckbo's *The Art of Home Landscaping* (published as *Landscaping for Western Living* in 1968), so that California became a utopia where every garden owner had access to the very best design ideas. Inspiration was found in the European avant-garde especially, and the works of Jean Arp, Joan Miró, Moholy-Nagy and Kandinsky were drafted into the garden in the exploration of new spatial perceptions. The garden had become a box of sensual tricks, to be opened and analysed in all its forms and functions.

It was well enough to find inspiration in abstract or constructive artists, but conveying the appearance of the modern garden was crucial, and difficult. For the embryonic landscape architect a drawing style was a means of self-expression, a design criterion, as well as a message: as students or assistants they spent hours thinking themselves into the space on the paper in front of them, organizing requirements and juggling solutions. Designers' 'doodles' were developed into a graphic vocabulary to express the actions and reactions of a person in a garden (see p. 92). The functional sketches were allied to the abstract inspirations, the experience of multi-dimensional space rather than merely a flat plane,

and something of the 'inherent nature' of trees, shrubs and hedges was included. The result was a very expressive garden drawing, produced on axonometric or isometric principles: this was much more than a garden plan, it was a statement that the modern garden had found its identity in the arms of modern art.

The modern garden in prairie and desert

The landscape profession naturally had a vested interest in the belief that the future was in the vast 'urban recreational environment'. They invented the 'view garden' – not the French modernist motif of a platform for viewing from, but as an entity in the view itself. If landscape design's purpose was 'to establish a scale relation between man and the large landscape he sees' then 'the view garden relates man to the landscape literally; the enclosed, self-sufficient garden must supply a space and material experience comparable to that relationship in quality'.[24] This is the justification for the professionals' learning to design small spaces, but there were other pressures upon the Californian dream which were to have a profound effect upon the garden. The first, in a word, was *water*: the discovery of an environmental consciousness in the 1960s meant that California was soon to become riven, north from south, by arguments over the rising demands for water, and gardens were named as greedily anti-social devices (after golf courses – deemed to be the greater social and commercial necessity). The dreaded shortage of water gave impetus to the environmentalists, a burgeoning wing of the design professions: there had long been a 'natural habitat' wing of the modern garden movement, and this had now reached California.

In its metaphorical journeying from innovatory New England and along the wagon trails to the west, the modern garden had acquired an air of northern naturalism, an almost defiant pride in nature and natural elements, given verity by so many Scandinavian and Nordic immigrants and found apposite to the mid-western grasslands. The modern garden never forgot its northern blood: Garrett Eckbo's life had been changed by

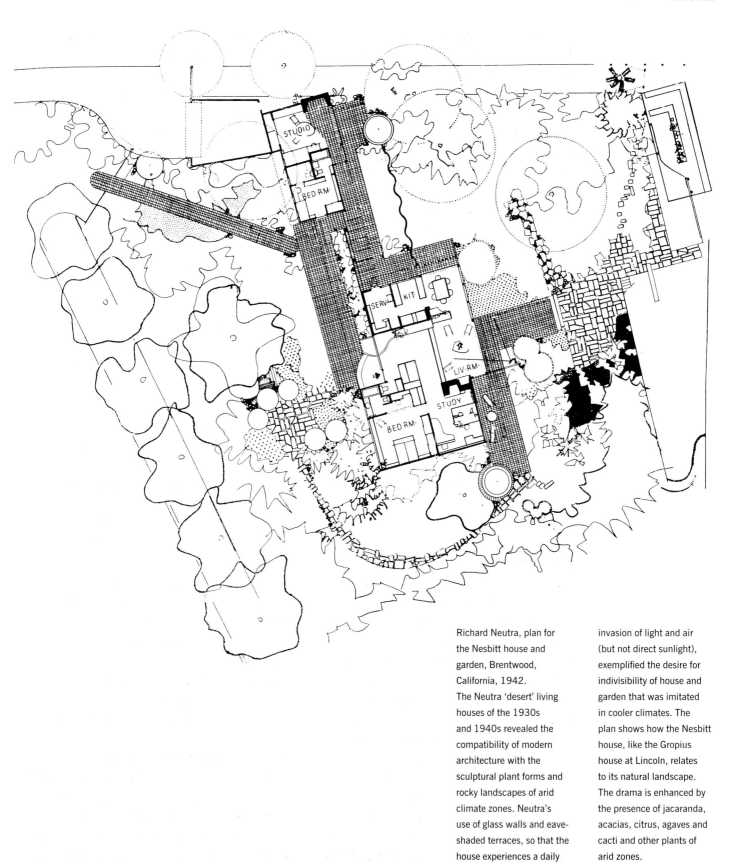

Richard Neutra, plan for the Nesbitt house and garden, Brentwood, California, 1942.
The Neutra 'desert' living houses of the 1930s and 1940s revealed the compatibility of modern architecture with the sculptural plant forms and rocky landscapes of arid climate zones. Neutra's use of glass walls and eave-shaded terraces, so that the house experiences a daily invasion of light and air (but not direct sunlight), exemplified the desire for indivisibility of house and garden that was imitated in cooler climates. The plan shows how the Nesbitt house, like the Gropius house at Lincoln, relates to its natural landscape. The drama is enhanced by the presence of jacaranda, acacias, citrus, agaves and cacti and other plants of arid zones.

Luis Barragán, San Cristobal Stables, near Mexico City, 1967–68. The architectural splendour only serves to emphasize the sacred presence of water, source of life for man, beast and vegetation, which is at the heart of Barragán's inspiration.

six months in Oslo when he was nineteen, the Saarinens settled at Cranbrook in Michigan, dreaming of the birch trees of Hvittrask, and there was the founder member of the Prairie School of design, Jens Jensen.

Jens Jensen (1860–1951) stands like some Viking ghost at the modern garden party. The older he became the more he cultivated the bold Viking image, with flowing hair and moustache, and a silver wolf clasp on his neckscarf; his clients were duly intimidated.[25] Born in Jutland, Denmark, he arrived in Chicago when he was twenty-six, taking a job as a gardener for the city Parks department; he was 'struck by the prairie, that great sea of grasses blazing with acres of purple phlox and burnt-orange rudbeckia still (then) surrounding the city. During his fourteen years as a gardener… he made regular weekend trips to the prairie and the wooded bluffs of the North Shore.' His familiarity with the entire Midwestern range of plants, his sensitivity to their individual personalities, to their growth habits, and their comparisons in the wild, all date to this long apprenticeship.[26] He was only interested in enhancing the glorious landscape that nature had given America (which so few others seemed to see) – he planted native trees, sugar maples and elms, 'skirted' with flowering dogwood, shadblow, plum, redbud, ninebark and many others; his ground coverings were of blue *Phlox divaricata,* yellow lady's slipper, purple violets, *Cornus canadensis* and *Trillium grandiflorum* 'signature flowers of the northern woods'.[27] Jensen represented the ecologically conscious designers, before such a term had truly been invented: in *The Prairie Spirit in Landscape Gardening*, Wilhelm Miller had identified 'the movement founded on the fact that one of the greatest assets which any country or natural part of it can have is a strong national or regional character'.[28]

Jensen's client list was impressive (it included Edsel Ford and his wife Eleanor Clay) and he was Frank Lloyd Wright's chosen collaborator. He had been most involved with Wright's early houses: he worked on the Coonley House, and on the garden for the Sherman M. Booth house 1910–11, when his office was in the same building as Wright's. He was a frequent visitor to Taliesin, and was inspired by it to found his own

school, The Clearing, in Door County, Wisconsin, which still survives.[29]

In the 1920s Wright's communing with his own ancestral landscape in Spring Green, Wisconsin, had been extended to the searing sunlight and rocky cactusland of Arizona's southwestern desert. Wright regarded Taliesin West as the 'second chapter' of his development – and his westward drift found an innate response in the American psyche; at about the time of Jensen's death in 1951 the 'prairie' gave way to the 'desert' as the new environmental focus. In her analysis of Wright as an 'Architect of Landscape', Anne Whiston Spirn suggests that he romanticized both prairie and desert in that 'he spent the most pleasant seasons in each' not contending with their rounded natures.[30] She also proposes a fundamental source of disagreement between Wright and Jensen, that while the latter treated natural habitats and native plants as the authority for design, Wright, the more modern prophet, became the constructivist sculptor-architect, seeking the symbolic form or 'inner nature'. Spirn notes Wright and Jensen's differences over concepts of 'nature', and acknowledges that although they remained friends, they did not work together after Wright's return from Europe. At Taliesin West, he seems to have worked like a sculptor, constantly revising and changing, refining the physical surroundings. Spirn writes of being in the building and looking out to distant views 'following the plane of interior floor to exterior terrace, then outside, tracing the line of walls and roofs as they slid into terrain in a fusion of building and earth'. Wright 'captured' the landscape into his house, into the experience of moving through it, as through the Japanese stroll garden 'with its twisting, turning path, views concealed then revealed (to impart) a sense of flux and mutability'.[31]

Gradually the desert became the most desirable place to live (seasonally) for the American avant-garde. The deep yearning for 'Arabia deserta' found an all-American response especially from architects whose 'pure' buildings found repose in this naked, arid landscape. Luis Barragán and Roberto Burle Marx, in Mexico and South America, extended the triumph of the modern garden into the farthest sun-drenched regions.

dan **kiley**

miller house *columbus, indiana, usa*

Dan Kiley was born in 1912 in Roxbury, Massachusetts, and his childhood was divided between Boston and his grandparents' farm in New Hampshire. If there is one book a child in that part of the world should read it is, of course, Henry David Thoreau's *Walden*: Kiley was not a bookish boy, but he read this book over and over again, and it gave him his understanding of the American landscape, and his place in it. He graduated from high school in the worst depression year, 1930, but found a job as 'dogsbody' for the landscape architect Warren Manning, a parks man of the old school, who had worked with Frederick Law Olmsted. Kiley enrolled on the Harvard landscape course at the same time as James Rose and Garrett Eckbo. These three were the revolutionaries at Harvard, who virtually invented modern landscape architecture.

Kiley's garden for the Irwin Miller house in Columbus, Indiana, the house designed by Eero Saarinen and Kevin Roche, contributes to one of the most sublime masterpieces of modern design. Irwin Miller was a patron in the grand manner, determined that his city should display the very best in modern design, and on a private basis, that his own house and garden should subscribe to his ideal centre of excellence.

The first thing that Kiley did was to act as if he was the architect: he set Saarinen and Roche's constructional plan of the house into a grid and analysed its proportions, which he used as the basis for his spatial divisions. The garden of the Miller house thus becomes a celebration of its own chief ornament, and every avenue and lawn subscribes to the delight. At Harvard, the triumvirate of Eckbo, Kiley and Rose had raged against the flatly picturesque nature of design: they had longed for involvement in the spaces, for a fully rounded appreciation of proportions, textures, light and shade. The Miller garden is Kiley's definitive answer to their questions, the most powerful statement of how to design with ground covers, trees, shrubs, space and light.

Kiley is the supreme master of the modern garden, and he has created many small-scale works in a long career of landscape design: these include the Philosopher's garden and others on the campus of Rockefeller University, New York, the Gregory house, Wayzata, Minnesota, the Lear residence, Brentwood, California, the Lehr residence, Miami Beach, Florida, and the Kusko house, Williamstown, Massachusetts.

TOP LEFT
Horse chestnuts, symbolic trees for Le Corbusier and the Saarinens, were part of the original planting beside the drive, with low blocks of yew as their foil.

TOP RIGHT
The floor plane of the rectangular house is 'pulled' into the garden by Kiley's twenty-five foot plinth surround, creating sunny or shaded outdoor spaces.

BOTTOM LEFT
The swimming pool enclosure surrounded by ten foot high yew hedges.

BOTTOM RIGHT
The path to the swimming pool, with the gate by Alexander Girard.

'No contours or rebel trees to dilute the purity of formal expression': the avenue of honey-locust brings forth 'qualities of colour, texture and light that no other tree would do'.

RIGHT
The avenue looking north, towards Henry Moore's *Seated Woman*.

BELOW
Shade from the honey-locusts and weeping beeches next to the sitting terrace.

OPPOSITE
The house, weeping beeches and honey-locust avenue: to the left the shade gives way to the open sunny meadow.

Henry Moore's *Seated Woman* evolves through differing perspectives: across the mown grass of the meadow (opposite); through the grove of redbud (below); from one of two regularly planted orchards, used as sculptural mass in the overall layout.

FOLLOWING PAGES
Moore's *Seated Woman* through irrigated haze, from the edge of the redbud grove. (above right) The honey-locust avenue looking south to the closing of the vista by Jacques Lipchitz's bas relief. (bottom right) Dawn over one of the two orchards.

roberto **burle marx**

brazil

The most seriously committed plantsman of the modern movement was undoubtedly Roberto Burle Marx (1909–94). He was a passionate artist and patriot, and a knowledgeable botanist and plant collector: his work occupies a place of admiration, if not adoration, amongst the cognoscenti of modern art. However Burle Marx's determination to work and live in his native Brazil, and his devotion to his own landscape, have set him apart.

When he was nineteen his family spent eighteen months in Berlin, where he took a deep draught of modernism, and made his devastating discovery of the wonders of Brazilian exotics, such as palms, cycads, aloe, philodendrons and cactus, in the glasshouses of the Dahlem Botanic Garden. He made drawings of the plants, and passed his first modern hurdle immediately, realizing that 'one may think of a plant as a brushstroke… but one must never forget that it is an individual living plant'.[1]

In 1930 he began to study painting, architecture and landscape design in Rio de Janeiro, with Lucio Costa and Oscar Niemeyer and other pioneers of Brazilian modernism: from the first he was the artist-plantsman, an equal among the others who were architects. He used exotic natives culled and propagated from his own plant-hunting expeditions into the interior with his first commission, the roof garden of the Alfredo Schwartz house in Rio de Janeiro in 1932, a severe white box of a building (designed by Costa and Warchavchik) with a garden of paved white squares, interspersed with white concrete roundels filled with flowers.

Burle Marx's first job was as Keeper of Parks in Pernambuco, and he spent a few years in Recife restoring native plants to parks and gardens, learning a great deal about the plants from close contact. He won the appreciation of his peers with his 1948 garden for Odette Monteiro at Correias, Rio, where a sinuous pathway unrolls across a moving gardenscape of green mounds, sweeping beds of coleus in vibrant colours, punctuated with stands of strelitzia, fringed with trees and capped with blue sky.

In 1949 Burle Marx found and purchased the Sitio St Antonio da Bica in Campo Grande which was to be his home, with extensive nurseries and a great plant collection, for the rest of his life. His was an early voice for conservation of habitats and many rarities bear his name. He was the epitome of a modern movement environmentalist.

TOP LEFT AND BOTTOM RIGHT
Ministry of Education and Health, Rio de Janeiro, designed in the 1930s and now restored.

TOP RIGHT AND BOTTOM LEFT
Burle Marx used exotic ground patterns in hard and soft textures; the planted waves are an alternative to the spectacular paving with which he edged Rio's famous Copacabana beach.

LEFT AND BELOW

Flamengo Park, Rio de Janeiro, around the Museum of Modern Art, a landfill project on the edge of the harbour developed in the 1950s.

OPPOSITE

Courtyard and atrium projects were often designed to be seen from above, with the added excitement of plants climbing walls and structures as if to meet the observer.

Bold designs on a large scale, using geometrically contained water features. Burle Marx – like Erich Mendelsohn – also believed in clothing buildings in luxuriant flowers and foliage.

Three views of the garden
for the Hospital da Lagoa
(Sul America), Rio de
Janeiro. Burle Marx's
gardens are like his abstract
paintings laid on the
ground. He was uniquely
skilled as both painter
and plantsman.

dressing the **modern garden**

Plants are to the [garden] designer what words are to the conversationalist. Anyone can use words. Anyone can use plants; but the fastidious will make them sparkle with aptness.[1]

James Rose, 1938

To the modern movement theorists plants were not only a matter of form and colour. As with materials, they possessed inherent characteristics and qualities of their own but with livelier intimations. There was also a lingering concern that plants could be regarded as mere ornament, a 'crime' according to Adolf Loos, and so in order to justify the modern movement's embrace of the persistently green and growing elements in design, some more empathetic connection was required.

CIRCLE (1937) included a note on 'biotechnics' (plant technology) by Karel Houzik, which acknowledged Sir Joseph Paxton's observations on the structural strengths of the great water-lily leaves of *Victoria amazonica*, and paid yet more attention to Maurice Maeterlinck's *L'Intelligence des Fleurs* of 1907. Maeterlinck (1862–1949), the Belgian dramatist whose *Pelleas et Mélisande* was the source for

Pietro Porcinai, Giardino della Società Nariana, Fiesole, Florence.

Debussy's opera, was a philosopher-naturalist, a bee-keeper and an influential Symbolist with French poets Stéphane Mallarmé and Paul Verlaine. His *Life of the Bee* (1901) was folllowed by his observations of flowers, which appeared in English translation by Alexander Teixeira de Mattos, among other essays, in 'Life and Flowers' published in London in 1907. Maeterlinck insisted that his essay contained no more than botanists' elementary observations, but of course in the mind and hands of such a philosopher they assumed new power. He noted that no plant is wholly devoid of wisdom and ingenuity, and all exert themselves to the utmost of their abilities in an attempt to conquer the globe. The root, condemned to immobility and darkness, has one fixed idea: to grow, to bloom, invoke wings and fly. He discusses lowly medicks and clovers and the intricacies of hooks, whorls and spirals that they invent in their craving for space, as well as the flying machines of thistledown and propellers and screws of ash and maple (in 1907 all on the frontiers of aeronautical invention). He ascribes 'a prudent and quick intelligence' to a laurel

growing from a seed caught in a crevice in a steep bank, which finds a foothold, grows horizontally then balances itself with a contorted trunk, a knotted elbow with 'all the free and conscious genius of the plant… centred around that vital knot'. He makes a miniature saga of *Nigella damascena*, love-in-a-mist, growing wild beneath the olive trees in southern France, with five extremely long pistils grouped in the centre of the azure crown 'like five queens clad in green gowns, haughty and inaccessible' – and around them crowding the throng of their lovers, the stamens. Now begins the drama without words, of motionless waiting – 'hours pass that are flowers' years' – the nigellas fade, petals fall, and the pride of the great queens seems at last to give way so that a given moment and in a symmetrical movement ('comparable with the harmonious parabolas of a five-fold jet of water') they bend backwards and cull the dust 'of the mystical kiss on the lips of their humble lovers'.[2]

Maeterlinck's magicianship allowed plants into modern thinking as more or less 'honorary humans'. Complementary ways of thinking came from other

The planting designs of Brazilian Roberto Burle Marx, the most influential plantsman of the modern movement, recall his skill as an abstract painter: his gardens become abstract art on the ground on a vast scale. He used 'elements of nature, mineral and vegetable, as materials for plastic construction as other artists worked on canvas with paint and brush.'

directions, from a curiosity and interest in Chinese and Japanese plants and gardens, and from the horticultural sensitivities of a Swiss nurseryman, Henri Correvon, who had been trained at the Edinburgh Botanic Garden under the great Sir Isaac Bayley Balfour (1853–1922), who had visited both China and Japan and made Edinburgh's rock garden the finest in Britain.

Henri Correvon (whose brother Fernand was a landscape architect in Geneva) was an alpinist and an Anglophile: he had many gardening friends in Britain, he contributed to Robinson's *The Garden*, and though he had an intimate knowledge of the plants that were at home in his Alpine nurseries, he seemed to revel in larger species that grew well in softer conditions, with a fine appreciation of forms. In *The Alpine Flora* (published in English translation by E. W. Clayforth in 1912), Correvon describes 'the stately groups of ornamental rhubarbs', the 'architectural masses' of monkshoods, knotweeds (especially *Polygonum molle*), the golden-orbed doronicum, senecios and ferns 'most manifold' in Lord Henry Bentinck's rock garden at Kirkby Lonsdale, Cumbria. He also pays attention to acanthus, artichokes, cardoons, onopordons, thistles and eryngiums. *The Alpine Flora* was illustrated with a collection of startling watercolours by Philippe Robert (1881–1930), with anemones, sedums, violas, gentians, saxifrages arranged upon the pages with a boldness that surpasses even Charles Rennie Mackintosh's flower paintings and looks to futurist textile designs. (Robert was dismissed briefly in Wilfrid Blunt's 'The Art of Botanical Illustration' for a 'certain primitive gaiety' in these drawings.)[3] The very presence of Robert's illustrations in the book confirms that Correvon saw each plant with its individual qualities, rather than as propagated masses for profit. His native understanding of plants that were grown in rocky habitats (which finds an immediate response in the Chinese and Japanese reverence for mountains and rocks) seemed to flourish amongst the more exuberant growth in the gardens of his English friends. Correvon coined the term 'formes architecturales' to describe plants that possessed inherent qualities for the modern designer: the acanthus, the wreath of Corinthian capitals, had a place of honour.

LANDSCAPE AND GARDEN

SPRING 1934

ISSUED UNDER THE AUSPICES OF THE INSTITUTE OF LANDSCAPE ARCHITECTS

Edited by RICHARD SUDELL

Avant-garde cover by Sylvia Bergin for the journal of the Institute of Landscape Architects, 1934.

It is possible to highlight other exemplary 'designer's plants'. The sword-like yucca and New Zealand flax and sword-like miniatures, *Iris pallida*: others that could hold their dignity in stony expanses, the big-leaved ivy, *Hedera colchica*, or the personable mound of *Viburnum davidii*: further magnificent leaf shapes included those of the suave hostas, rounded 'elephant's ear' bergenia, and the almost-human handed palmates, from maples, through figs and virginia creepers, to tiarella and alchemilla. Some plants hold themselves extraordinarily upright, the graceful Solomon's Seal, the big euphorbias and agapanthus: some appear aggressive, the prickly eryngiums and mahonias (was ever a plant better-named than *Eryngium giganteum*, 'Miss Willmott's ghost'?), and some were pliable and friendly, *Senecio greyi* and the benevolent sedums, house-leeks and stonecrops. Many herbs, especially rosemary and thymes, were treasured for homely association with the kitchen garden and back door, and water plants were beloved of modern designers, as was water itself. Even the humble lamium was prized for its leaf splashed with silver which glowed in the gloom, and the equally modest vinca, or periwinkle, approved for the green sheen of its foliage.

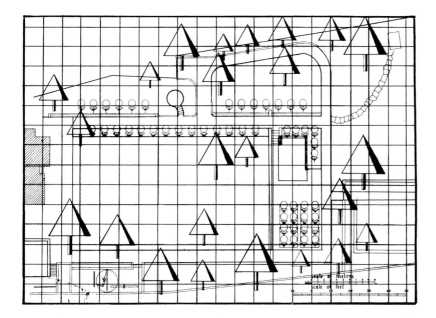

Otto Valentien, plan for a small garden in Stuttgart (1930). Valentien, chief designer for the Berlin horticulturists Spaeth in the 1920s and subsequently in private practice, felt he was developing 'a new type of garden'. The house is left of the plan, facing south; the garden has 'clear spaces with stretches of grass and good straight walks' and a pavilion open to the view, with screens of glass for shelter.

The concept of 'formes architecturales', of plants with personality and characteristics that could be exploited for design purposes, was adopted by architects and garden designers with a modern sympathy. In 1925 Mien Ruys photographed a simple square pool, enhanced by the elegant gathering of astilbes and rodgersias, highly approved 'designer's plants'. Many modern gardens of the late 1920s and early 1930s sported variable arrangements of simple squares, each square filled with child-like rows of tulips or a single branching shrub: the square, often made by 'left-out' paviours, was a practical and flexible means of planting vegetables or ornamental plants, but this simplicity also isolated the plant as an object of reverence. The cover of the 1934 spring issue of *Landscape and Garden*, 'issued under the auspices of the Institute of Landscape Architects', showed of a drawing by Sylvia Bergin, a 'worm's eye view' of seven crocus and three subordinate and leafless trees bending in the wind and rain of an April shower. With some wit, the crocus was imbued with all the style and grace of a poplar tree.

Such minimalism was obviously derided by horticulturists and nursery owners who saw a dangerous drop in the market for plants. But the sensibilities of Maeterlinck and Correvon were only the beginning of modern planting design. In the 1930s the philosophies of Chinese and Japanese gardens were more accessible and desirable to modern theorists: Tunnard scornfully rejected European garden style history, in the manner of Le Corbusier, but was only too eager to turn to the sympathetic mysteries of the East. The Chinese had spent centuries refining their native flora into the spiritual symbols that they cherished in their gardens: the virtuous bamboo that bent in the storm but never broke, the herbaceous peonies and the even more revered tree peony, the moutan, the chrysanthemums cultivated for a thousand years, and their favourite trees, the catalpa, sophora 'the pagoda tree', paulownia, and the weeping willow, symbolic of pliable feminine grace. In her memoir 'Ancient Melodies', Su Hua recalls the 'wise and loving' family gardener Lao Chou at their home in Peking in the early twentieth century: as a girl she was allowed to go with him to the city market, they would collect parings of horses' hoofs from the blacksmith to make into a broth for feeding the orchids, and they bought offal to bury near the roses. Lao Chou took her to visit 'a white-haired old countryman who had been head gardener at the Summer Palace in the days of the old Empress Tzu Hsi – whose touching concern for the welfare of her plants had been balanced by a remarkable indifference towards human beings'. As it was never known which of the pavilions the Empress would frequent on any given day, all the pavilions had to be daily filled with fresh flowers, and she demanded that they include all the blossoms – many kinds of prunus, the peonies, roses, chaenomeles (quince) and lilies – that had figured in paintings and on scrolls, and these were not to be the 'curled or trained flowers' found in the market but those grown in her own gardens. The aged imperial gardener had a two-hundred-year-old wisteria, 'its trunk like a dragon rising from the sea', and a three-hundred-year-old lilac, like 'a woman dancing with a beautiful motion'. He tended these gems 'with infinite love and care, following a body of gardeners' lore which had been passed down orally from generation to generation. He drew from this rich and ancient tradition not only the shrewd practical details of horticulture – 'what oils to apply to rotting roots, and how to propagate fruit trees… but also special feeling, inspired by the Taoist beliefs, about a gardener's relationship with his plants'.[4]

It was as if the modern designers, adrift in the turbulent unknown of the 1930s, yearned for the ancient Chinese gardening wisdom, along with the plants: plants that brought these mystical associations into the modern design repertory, not only lilacs, wisteria and catalpa, but (as illustrated by Gordon Cullen in Tunnard's *Gardens in the Modern Landscape*) the twiggy *Viburnum fragrans,* the spreading Chinese juniper, *J. chinensis Pfitzeriana*, the soothing Chinese witch-hazel, *Hamamelis mollis*, and startling white-stemmed *Rubus Giraldianus*, brought from China in 1907.[5]

The Chinese symbolism was overlaid, and sometimes confused with, a Bernard Leach-inspired knowledge of Japanese gardens, which tended to be on a smaller scale, courtyard gardens that were miniature landscapes, and therefore more accessible in every way. The studied arrangements of stones – the worshipping stone, the waiting stone, the guardian stone – and miniature trees of the Shin or So styles – the tree of upright spirit or the distancing pine – and the austere raked sand of the Zen temple gardens, brought timeless messages to the soul, but they had two main meanings for modern designers. The first, which Tunnard also wrote of as the phenomenon of Japanese art, was 'the feeling for a spiritual quality in inanimate objects… the waving of a branch in obedience to the wind, the refreshing and purifying flow of a surging stream – these things were significant to the landscape painter and gardener alike, and were loved by them as being near to their own experience'.[6]

The second clear lesson from these gardens was to observe the dignified equality of materials. The raked sand was the symbolic ground for two or three rocks and two or three precious plants; the flat So-style courtyard garden of Mr Yamoaka in Kyoto (illustrated in *The Studio*, 'Modern Gardens', 1927) has three stones and a lantern 'of rare shape' grouped around a many-branched tree, and a guardian deity, a stone ram. There are other delicate trees, the smallest of which seems to be a camellia, but there is the essential equality in earth, stone, foliage and flowers. No 'great waves of vegetation' or 'barbaric massings of colour' – for which Tunnard

cursed English gardens – but an elegant respect for nature. Interesting leaf shapes, colours and textures, elegant form and plants with the ability to produce decorative autumn fruits were of much greater importance than mere flowers. These plants had to be tolerant of dry sun and/or wet shade, hardy to survive in predominantly man-made environments of paved courts and terraces, roof gardens and wall footings. They had also to be on parade every day of the year, with no seasonal respites as in the variable 'rooms' of older

Plants with personality: good nurseries provided sketches of essential forms and habits. These are from a 1960s catalogue for Scotts' Nurseries of Merriott, Somerset.

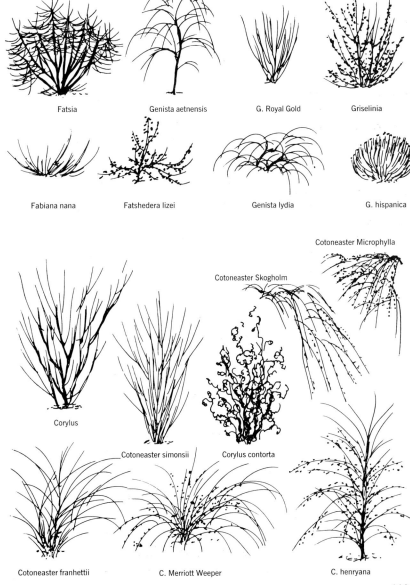

Fatsia

Genista aetnensis

G. Royal Gold

Griselinia

Fabiana nana

Fatshedera lizei

Genista lydia

G. hispanica

Corylus

Cotoneaster simonsii

Corylus contorta

Cotoneaster Skogholm

Cotoneaster Microphylla

Cotoneaster franhettii

C. Merriott Weeper

C. henryana

gardens. *Gardens in the Modern Landscape* had illustrations of these plants by Gordon Cullen – they included the approved plants for modern patios and terraces: *Vinca major elegantissima* (golden periwinkle), *Pachysandra terminalis,* hebes, ivies, *Fatsia japonica,* many berberis and contoneaster (*C. horizontalis*), bamboos, New Zealand flax, viburnums, hostas, euphorbias, *Tiarella cordifolia* and grasses and herbs.

Fewer plants, but greater care for those you have, was the resulting message to modern plantsmen: a long and respectful co-existence of feeding, pruning, training and enjoying – of wisteria, forsythia, camellia, cherry, miniature pines and cut-leaved maples, all of which were being enthusiastically planted in 1930s gardens. Japanese gardens had been featured regularly in the West at least since the 1890s, when the *Gardeners' Chronicle* had printed an amazed account of an imperial chrysanthemum exhibition in Tokyo and *The Studio* 'Gardens and Gardening' volumes after 1927 included Japan in their gardener's world. Charles Holme's editorial in 1936 looked forward to the revelation of 'modernism' in gardens. In 1940, in a volume mostly devoted to wartime gardening, he included a long retrospective in admiration of the Japanese arts of flower arranging and painting, of how long years of reverence and care for an old plum tree or *Chimonanthus fragrans* (*praecox*), 'winter-sweet', gave beauty and meaning to paintings. Within a year the world war had intervened: Japan's entry into the war with the attack on Pearl Harbor in 1941 marked the end of this association for the next twenty years.

The most influential plantsman of the modern movement was undoubtedly Brazilian Roberto Burle Marx (1909–94). His gardens have been exhibited at the Museum of Modern Art in New York, and his name has been a byword for exciting modern planting design since his work was first heard of in London in the 1940s. He expressed his devotion to his native landscape using 'elements of nature, mineral and vegetable, as materials for plastic construction as other artists worked on canvas with paint and brush'. Although his tropical and sub-tropical planting have not been adapted effectively to the temperate world, in his lifetime he figured perhaps too

prominently as a national icon for this to be possible. When one considers that the French Impressionist painter Claude Monet's own garden at Giverny only really received serious attention in the last decade of the twentieth century, with the dreadful time-lag in the world of gardening reputations Burle Marx's time may be yet to come.

Designers' plants

With the outbreak of the Second World War, cultural sympathies in America, and especially California, with the countries on the far side of the Pacific were abandoned. The subtleties of occult symbolism, the quasi-human attributes of plants and the inherent qualities of materials were no longer studied. In occupied Europe the talk of *l'intelligence des fleurs* and biotechnics was hushed to a whisper – or the knowledge directed to nefarious scientific ends – and in Britain, one suspects, if Hitler had flaunted a pansy in his buttonhole, the whole viola species would have been jettisoned from gardens. From 'formes architecturales' to German naturalism (or wild gardens) the pioneer voices were silenced: in the aftermath, the division by the Iron Curtain, many of them would be heard no more.

The result was, in the post-war decade, that North American and British designers and academics, with inspiration from Roberto Burle Marx, constructed a fresh palette of approved plants which were shorn of their philosophic and cultural 'roots' and simply labelled 'designers' plants'. The designers in question were almost exclusively landscape architects – the approved plants were classified for students of landscape architecture – but the plants they purloined (and to some extent debased in monotonous public landscapes) were those of the garden, the favourites already identified by Henri Correvon and others, the plantsmen of both the East and West.

Plants for the modern garden were reclassified: they were extracted from their ecological niches, their climatic regions and soil types and reorganized according to situation – the roof garden or terrace, for dry or damp shade, full sun, exposure to wind or salt spray, for the flower box or other containers, or any of the micro-climatic computations that are created in a garden. Instead of their botanical family connections, they were re-aligned by use: ground cover, climbers and ramblers, spiky 'accent' plants or low-growing mounds, such as the classic *Viburnum davidii,* a modern favourite. Plant characteristics, as newly seen, were overwhelmingly visual – evergreen foliage, grey and silver leaves, ferny, variegated or prickly personalities of varying size and habit of growth – loose, compact, prostrate or upright. The strength of personality was appreciated on a rising scale when seen as a habit of growth: the spider-like flowers of the (Chinese) witch-hazel, *Hamamelis mollis* or *H. japonica*, ranked below the amazing contorted hazel, *Corylus avellana 'Contorta'*. Above these were the exotics, feats of cultivation as well as structure, such as

the cordyline or Chusan palm advocated for warm and sheltered courtyards by Christopher Tunnard. Modern plantsmen loved the unusual and strange, but they also loved the whole plant, the whole time: spring shoots, leaves and flowers, seed heads, frost-sculpted foliage, and forms cloaked in snow were equally appreciated.

The redefinition of designers' plants was part of an educative process: the fresh start of the late 1940s seemed to echo Gropius's and the other pioneers' rejections of the past of the early 1920s. The categories suggested by Eckbo, Kiley and Rose (see displayed quote on p. 122) – 'form, height at maturity, rate of growth, hardiness, soil requirements, deciduousness, colour, texture and time of bloom' – added to the possible or desirable uses meant that the landscape books and many plant catalogues were cluttered with complex lists

Modern planting at Noah's House, Bourne End, Buckinghamshire (now in Berkshire), 1930, by Colin Lucas. The garden features simple geometry, concrete and highly textured plants.

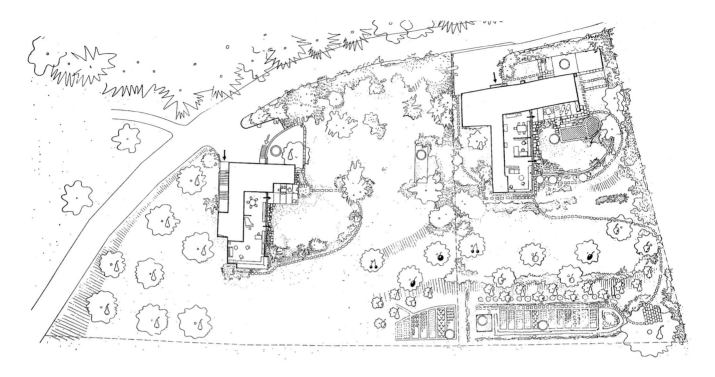

Site plan for two modern detached houses, carefully screened from each other, by Max Haefeli's practice in Zurich, 1931–34. The kitchen gardens are surrounded with fruit trees, boundaries planted with privet, viburnums, honeysuckles, shrub roses, cornus, hollies, philadelphus, hazels, thorns and other flowering shrubs, with oaks, poplars, birch, hornbeam, elders and willows complementing the surrounding native woodlands.

or graphs. This methodology for presenting approved plants confined them to a professional fiefdom, to a great extent denying them to the would-be modern gardener. There was no mystique (except in the system which attempted to explain a euphorbia or a eucalyptus to someone who had never met either) but equally there was no substitute for a close encounter with the plants. The simplest guides were the best: Scotts of Merriott pioneered the thumbnail sketches of form, Brenda Colvin's *Trees for Town and Country* had a clear message, and Beth Chatto's catalogues of the early 1960s *Unusual Plants* were innovatory. In her book *Garden Design* (1958), Sylvia Crowe gave two pages of lucid descriptions:

These attributes taken together – stature, form, pattern, texture and colour – add up to the plants's character; that indefinable personality which decides whether plants will look right together, and whether they will fill the particular place in the design for which they are intended. The best associations are between plants which have one element in common and another contrasted. Complete contrast in all elements can be used for special emphasis, but repeated too often the effect is restless, lacking the unity given by a connecting link of similarity.[8]

Plants have inherent quality, as do brick, wood, concrete, and other building materials, but their quality is infinitely more complex. To use plants intelligently, one must know, for every plant, its form, height at maturity, rate of growth, hardiness, soil requirements, deciduousness, colour, texture, and time of bloom. To express this complex of inherent quality, it is necessary to separate the individual from the mass, and arrange different types in organic relation to use, circulation, topography, and existing elements in the landscape.[7] Philosophy of Eckbo, Kiley and Rose, 1939

Peter Shepheard, the Moat Garden, the Festival of Britain, London, 1951. (above) Sketch of intended planting, with large and striking plants used as a visual as well as a physical barrier in the crowd circulation area.

BELOW
The plan, with labour-intensive details, such as labelling with Latin names and numbers of plants.

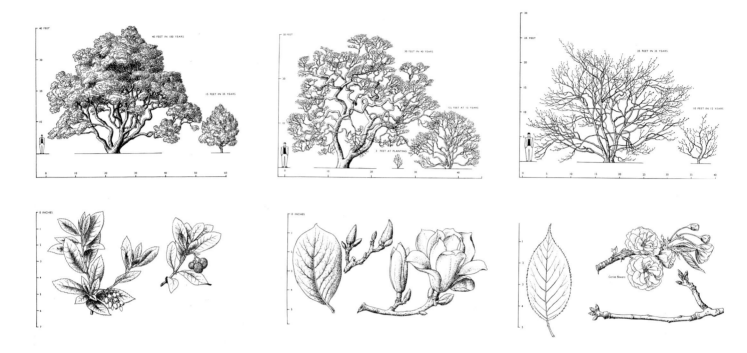

Designer's trees: *Arbutus unedo* (Strawberry tree), *Magnolia conspicua* (Yulan) and *Prunus serrulata sekiyama* (Japanese cherry) their essentials drawn by S. R. Badmin, for Brenda Colvin and Jacqueline Tyrwhitt's *Trees for Town and Country* (1947).

The yucca, recalled from Gertrude Jekyll, and the *Phormium tenax,* brought from New Zealand, were highly prized for bringing a desert-like spikiness into temperate gardens: they were to be 'used with discretion, usually as a point of emphasis… rising from a smooth surface or contrasting with a low rounded or horizontal form'. Large leaves were also admired: *Gunnera manicata,* rodgersias and rheums (the first two needing waterside planting) were all spectacular given space, and especially with the vertical contrast of a giant reed. The big, glaucous *Euphorbia wulfenii* ('an accent plant both in form and colour') should be complemented with other glaucous plants or left to stand alone 'related to architecture, at the corner of steps, or rising from the paving of a terrace'. Plate-like inflorescences were highly-prized, the flat, rich yellow heads of *Achillea eupatorium*, 'Gold Plate', the giant *Heracleum mantegazzianum* and *Viburnum rhytidophyllum,* all of which 'contain within themselves so fine a contrast of form that it is sufficient for them to stand alone, but they are also good as contrasts to low rounded masses or as stiffeners among plants of less determinate character'.[9]

The *Fatsia japonica* (*Aralia japonica*) was a great favourite, used against many courtyard walls, where the striking, large glossy green leaves looked best against a simple background. *Rhus typhina,* the stag's horn sumach, was similarly treasured for its velvety shoots and brilliant autumn colour (though many gardeners hate its suckering habits). The elegant spires of *Macleaya cordata, Thalictrum flavum glaucum,* the acanthus, and the 'thistly' cardoon, echinops and eryngiums 'all have strongly patterned foliage and a certain rigidity which gives stiffening and accent to less distinctive plants. But to be seen at their best they should stand out clearly as sculptural groups rising from a horizontal base, and either standing alone… or grouped with one contrasting form'. The example given is of the acanthus, the definitive 'architectural' plant contrasted with the enormous round leaves of *Hosta sieboldiana.*[10]

Sylvia Crowe's *Garden Design* deals expertly and at length on the subtleties of plant groupings and compatability, on colour and the effects of light and shade, and though she is a great admirer of Burle Marx and Lawrence Halprin, she does not confine herself to the modern garden, which she knew (or her publishers indicated) would not be popular with her readership. For infallibly modern advice and further expressions of the art of modern planting design, one must look to the designer and gardener whose brilliance amounts to genius, Mien Ruys (see Masterwork 7, pp. 142–53).

Designer's plants:

TOP

Hostas contrasted with ferns
grouped in Brenda Colvin's
tiny London garden in
Chelsea, in the 1930s.

BELOW

Big-leaved bergenia
contrasted with ferny
astilbe and spear-leaved
iris used for texture and
pattern in another early
Colvin garden in Hampshire.

The Cement and Concrete Association at Wexham Springs, Buckinghamshire, maintained fine demonstration gardens, designed in the 1960s: shown here is Sylvia Crowe's design and planting for the Town Garden, where formality gave way to a stream garden.

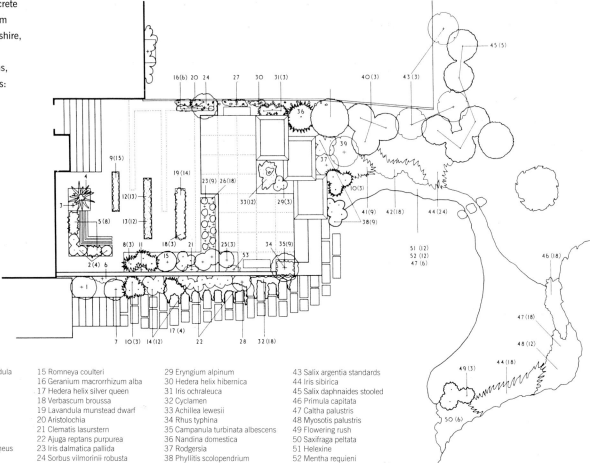

1 Cotoneaster hybrida pendula
2 Rosemarinus officinalis
3 Aralia chinensis
4 Yucca gloriosa
5 Convolvulus cnearum
6 Vitis coignetiae
7 Hydrangea quercifolia
8 Acanthus spinosus
9 Thymus serpyllum coccineus
10 Osmunda regalis
11 Clematis macrapetela
12 Acaena buchanini
13 Gentiana verna
14 Helleborus orientalis

15 Romneya coulteri
16 Geranium macrorrhizum alba
17 Hedera helix silver queen
18 Verbascum broussa
19 Lavandula munstead dwarf
20 Aristolochia
21 Clematis lasurstern
22 Ajuga reptans purpurea
23 Iris dalmatica pallida
24 Sorbus vilmorinii robusta
25 Tree peony
26 Dwarf pinks
27 Clematis spooneri
28 Hydrangea petiolaris

29 Eryngium alpinum
30 Hedera helix hibernica
31 Iris ochraleuca
32 Cyclamen
33 Achillea lewesii
34 Rhus typhina
35 Campanula turbinata albescens
36 Nandina domestica
37 Rodgersia
38 Phyllitis scolopendrium
39 Salix tortuosa
40 Sinarundinaria nitida
41 Iris kampferi
42 Primula florindae

43 Salix argentia standards
44 Iris sibirica
45 Salix daphnaides stooled
46 Primula capitata
47 Caltha palustris
48 Myosotis palustris
49 Flowering rush
50 Saxifraga peltata
51 Helexine
52 Mentha requieni
53 Clematis henryi

OPPOSITE, BOTTOM
Sylvia Crowe's Town Garden, Wexham Springs: pools and architectural plants.

FOLLOWING PAGES
Layout plan by Geoffrey Jellicoe and planting by Susan Jellicoe for the Terrace Garden. The insets – (left to right) 'iceberg' roses, euphorbia, poppies and peonies – are a reminder that flowers were not alien to the concrete setting of a modern garden.

John Nash (1893–1977): the modern artist-plantsman

All of John Nash's works, paintings, drawings, illustrations and wood engravings convey the modern artist's way of seeing the old world. In addition, as a gardener, illustrator of gardening books and a teacher of plant illustration, John Nash had an infallible eye for the essential 'personality' of a plant; the very fact that he drew a particular plant is often sufficient reason to include it in the modern gardener's repertory. The books with which Nash was associated have emphasized certain strands of the modern planting taste: *Poisonous Plants* (1927) and *Plants with Personality* (1938) both highlight the exotic, the rare (in gardens) and the

occasionally sinister aspects of vegetable characters. *Plants with Personality,* written with lively expertise by Patrick M. Synge (editor of the Royal Horticultural Society Journal and publications), illustrates horticultural ambitions in the modern idiom: there are chapters on insectivores, fly-pollinated arums and stapelias, South African strelitzias and gerberas, Chilean *Puya alpestris,* Mexican tiger-flowers and cacti and succulents. The penultimate chapter on 'Blues and Purples' features gentians, meconopsis, *Clematis* 'Jackmanii',' ceanothus, borage, ipomoea (Morning Glory), lithospermums, the humble *Iris unguicularis* (stylosa) amongst many others. Nash's drawings included the iris and the treasured *Tibouchina semi-decandra*, a velvety-purple aristocrat from Brazil – specimens were 'sent three times in ladies' stays boxes', Nash recalled, 'before a reasonable specimen sustained the post'.

John Nash's other illustrating partnerships, with Jason Hill (the pseudonym of Anthony Hampton) in *The Curious Gardener* (1932) and with Robert Gathorne-Hardy in *The Tranquil Gardener* (1958) and *The Native Garden* (1961) provide the modern plantsman with inspirational sources. Nash and his like-minded collaborators envisaged the essential 'idea' of a plant, as the modern way of seeing demanded: the truth was in the detail. At the close of his short autobiographical essay, *The Artist Plantsman,* written the year before he died, Nash remembered:

For nearly seventy years I have drawn plants for love or necessity and have never destroyed even slight sketches or notes in case they should be needed… In any case, I feel a slight pencil flourish even of part of a plant is more valuable than a photograph. The open innocent countenances of a Daisy or Anemone may seem easy to draw, but they too can prove to be a snare, and sometimes I prefer the hooded Labiates, helmeted Monkshood and Balsam, or the leering countenance of Foxglove and Penstemon.[11]

John Nash, from *The Tranquil Gardener* (1958) by Robert Gathorne-Hardy.

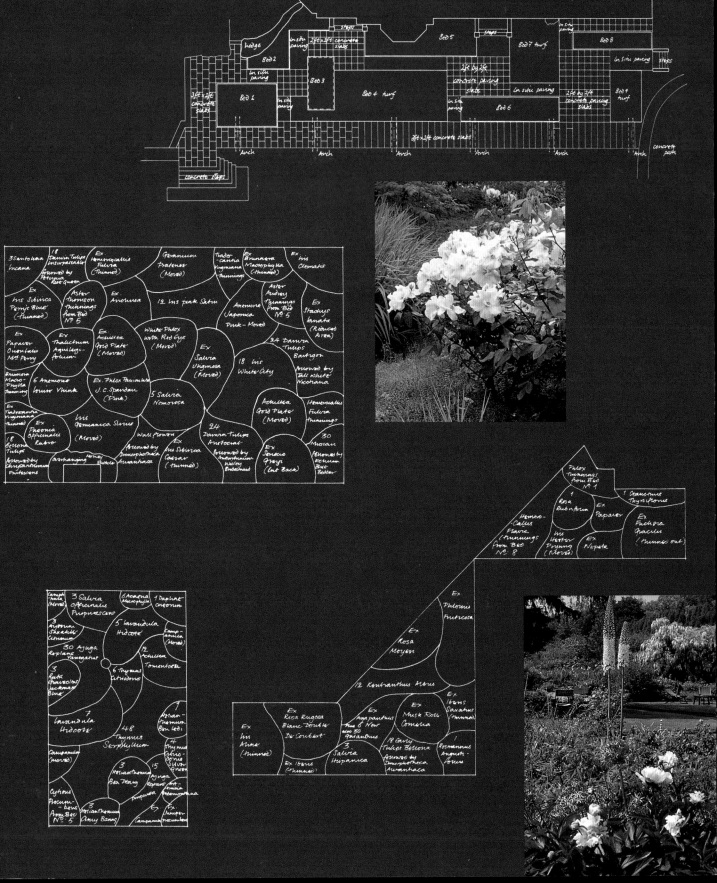

Top plan (garden layout):

hedge · Bed 2 · In situ paving · 2ft x 2ft concrete slabs · steps · Bed 5 · steps · Bed 7 turf · Bed 8
In situ paving · Bed 3 · In situ paving · 2ft by 2ft concrete paving · steps · In situ paving · Bed 9 turf · In situ paving · stairs
3ft x 2ft concrete slabs · Bed 1 · In situ paving · Bed 4 turf · In situ paving · Bed 6 · 2ft by 2ft concrete slabs
2ft x 2ft concrete slabs · concrete path
Arch · Arch · Arch · Arch · Arch · Arch
concrete slabs

Upper left bed plan:

3 Santolina Incana · 18 Darwin Tulips Insurpassable (followed by Petunia Rose Queen) · Hemerocallis Fulva (Thinned) · Geranium Pratense (Moved) · Trader-cantia Virginiana thinnings · Ex Brunnera Macrophylla (Thinned) · Ex Iris Clematis
Ex Iris Sibirica Perry's Blue (Thinned) · Aster Thomson thinnings from Bed No 5 · Ex Anchusa · 12 Iris pink Satin · Anemone Japonica Pink – Moved · Aster Audrey Thinnings from Bed No 5 · Ex Stachys lanata (Reduced Area)
Ex Papaver Orientalis Mrs Perry · Ex Thalictrum Aquilegi-folium · Ex Achillea Gold Plate (Moved) · White Phlox with Red Eye (Moved) · Ex Salvia Virginiana (Moved) · 18 Iris White City · 24 Darwin Tulips Bartigon (followed by Tall White Nicotiana)
Anemone Macro-Phylla thinning · 6 Anemone Louise Vmink · Ex Phlox Paniculata J. C. Spendan (Pink) · 5 Salvia Nemorosa · Achillea Gold Plate (Moved) · Hemerocallis Fulva thinnings
Ex Tradescantia Virginiana thinned · Ex Paeonia Officinalis Rubra (Moved) · Iris Germanica Sirius (Moved) · Wallflowers (followed by Dimorphotheca Aurantiaca) · Ex Iris Sibirica Caesar (thinned) · 24 Darwin Tulips Aristocrat (followed by Anchamium Wiley Bridesmaid) · Ex Senecio Greyi (cut back) · 30 Moccan (followed by Echium Blue Bedder)
18 Bottona Tulips (followed by Chrysanthemum Frutescens) · overhanging · Honey Suckle

Middle right small bed:

Phlox thinnings from Bed No 1 · 1 Ceanothus Thyrsiflorus · Ex Papaver · 1 Rosa Rubrifolia · Hemero-Callis Flava (thinnings from Bed No 8) · Iris Hector Pruning (Moved) · Ex Nepeta · Ex Fuchsia Gracilis (thinned out)

Lower left bed plan:

Campanula (Moved) · 3 Salvia Officinalis Purpurascens · 6 Acaena Macrophylla · 1 Daphne cneorum
3 Lippia Shrubbie Citriano · 5 Lavandula Hidcote · Camp-anula (Moved) · 12 Achillea Tomentosa · 30 Ajuga Reptans Variegatus · 3 Ruta Graveolens Jackman Blue · 6 Thymus Citriodorus
18 · 7 Lavandula Hidcote · 48 Thymus Serphyllum · 7 Helian-themum Ben Ledi · 4 Thymus Citrio-dorus Silver Queen
Campanula (Moved) · 3 Helianthemum Ben Dearg · 15 Ajuga Reptans · Campanula Rosemonthia
Cytisus Procum-bens from Bed No 5 · 3 Helianthemum Amy Baring · 3 Juniper · Campanula Procumbens

Lower right triangular bed:

Ex Phlomis Fruticosa · Ex Rosa Moyesii · 12 Kentranthus Albus · Ex Iris Saxatilis (thinned) · Ex Salvia Sclarea (thinned)
Ex Rosa Rugosa Blanc Double De Coubert · Ex Agapanthus plus 6 New also 30 Gardenias · Musk Rose Cornelia · 18 Early Tulips Bellona (followed by Dimorphotheca Aurantiaca) · Rosmarinus Angusti-folius
Ex Iris Aline (thinned) · 3 Salvia Hispanica · Ex Ibens (thinned)

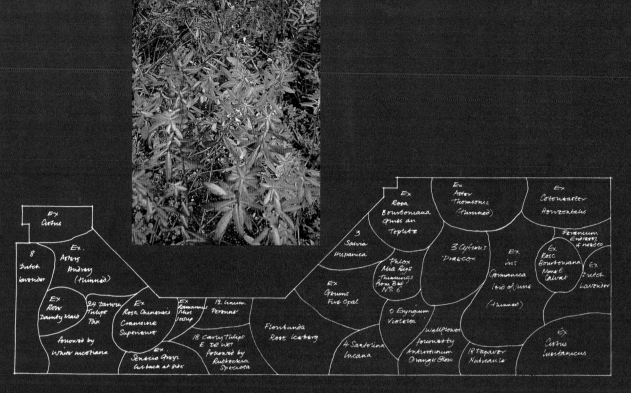

Top left bed plan

Ex Cistus

8 Dutch Lavender

Ex. Asters Audray (thinned)

Ex Rose Dainty Maid — followed by White nicotiana

24 Darwin Tulips Tax

Ex Rosa Chinensis Cramoisie Superieure

Ex Senecio Greyi cut back at side

Ex Ramanas Mrs Jessup

18 Early Tulips E DE WET followed by Rudbeckia Speciosa

12 Linum Perenne

Ex Geums Fire Opal

Floribunda Rose Iceberg

Top right bed plan

Ex Rosa Bourboniana Gloire an Teplitz

3 Salvia Hispanica

Ex Aster Thomsonic (thinned)

Ex Cotoneaster Horizontalis

Phlox Mia Ruys Thinnings from Bed No 6

3 Cytisus Praecox

Geranium Endressii 6 needed

Ex Iris Germanica Isle of June (thinned)

6 Rosa Bourboniana Mme E Calvat

Ex Dutch Lavender

6 Eryngium Violetta

Wallflower followed by Antirrhinum Orange Glow

4 Santolina Incana

18 Papaver Nudicaule

Ex Cistus Lusitanicus

Middle bed plan

4 Nepeta Mussini

Bergenia Cordifolia

Hemerocallis Flava (Moved)

Thalictrum Dipterocarpum from Bed No 6

Aster NB White Boy blue (Moved)

Ex Brunnera Macrophylla

Gypsophila Bristol Fairy

18 Darwin Tulips Insurpassable followed by Chrysanthemum Frutescens

6 Echinops from Bed No 2

Achillea Taygeta (Moved)

Ex Phlox Mia Ruys

Ex Rose Buff Beauty

Overhanging Yew

3 Bergenia Cordifolia

3 Santolina Incana

Ibens from Bed No 2

24 Early Tulips Brilliant Star followed by Antirrhinum Orange Glow

Tradescantia J.C. Weguelin (Moved)

Brunnera Macrophylla

Bottom bed plan

Existing Armeria Maritima

18 Early Tulips den De Wet Au in Persian Rose Queen

Ex Paeony

Tradescantia (Moved)

3 Verbascum Armstrong

8 Artemisia Ludoviciana

Ex Iris Sibirica

Ex Bergenia Cordifolia

6 Thalictrum Aquilegi folium

Ex Hemerocallis Dr Regel (thinned)

24 Darwin Tulips Apeldoorn followed by white top Chrysanthemum

1 Paeonia Whitley Major

Stachys lanata from Bed No 1

Ex Campanula Persicifolia

Paeony Lady A. Duff

Ex Iris Germaine Perthuis (thinned)

Papaver Orientalis Perrys White

Ex Helenium Autumnale Rubrum

Achillea Goto Plate (Moved)

Geranium Grossii (Moved)

Iris Senlac Thinnings

Geranium Endressii (Moved)

Phlox Frau Antoine Buchner (Moved)

Ex Achillea Goto Plate (thinned)

Ex Asters (thinned)

Ex Iris Germanica Senlac (thinned)

30 Darwin Tulips by Geranium Blue Bird

4 Kentranthus Atrococcinea

Aquilegia (Moved)

Bocconia Cordata (Moved)

Iris Aline Thinnings from Bed No 1

Aster NB Chequers (Moved)

Ex Sidalcea Rev Page Rose 18

Iris Pallida Dalmatica (Moved)

Iranthum Morris latifolia (Moved)

Lilac Flowers followed by Rudbeckia Speciota

Ibens from Bed No 1

24 Early Tulips Pink Beauty followed by Antirrhinum Wisley Bridesmaid

Papaver Orientalis Grossfurst Plus 6 Now

Phlox Mia Ruys (Moved)

Iris Dreamsinc Temperhoten

3 Verbascum Bronze

Iris Sibirica Caesar Thinnings from Bed No 1

3 Euphorbia Walteri

Ex Tradescantia J.C. Weguelin

Architectural plants
Acanthus spinosus
Agapanthus africanus (African lily)
Arundinaria (all bamboos)
Arundo donax (giant reed)
Cortaderia sellona (pampas grass)
Euphorbia wulfenii
Cynara cardunculus (cardoon)
Fatsia japonica
LEFT Heracleum mantegazzianum
Phormium tenax
Yucca (all)
Zantedeschia aethiopica

Introduced garden trees
RIGHT Liriodendron tulipifera (tulip tree)
Arbutus unedo (strawberry tree)
Parrottia persica
Acer griseum (paperbark maple)
Acer palmatum (purple vars.)
Acer platanoides vars.
Rhus typhina (sumach)
Cornus mas (cornelian cherry)
Catalpa bignonioides (Indian bean tree)
Magnolias (many)

Seaside plants
Crambe cordifolia
Hippophae rhamnoides
RIGHT, with cardoon, Limonium (sea lavender)
Pittosporum tenuifoilum
Rhamnus alaternus (buckthorn)
Tamarix gallica

Water plants
Aponogeton distachyos (water hawthorn)
Butomus umbellatus (flowering rush)
Caltha palustris (bog arum)
Cyperus longus (umbrella grass)
Iris kaempferi
LEFT Gunnera manicata
Juncus effusus spiralis (corkscrew rush)
Mentha aquatica (water mint)
Menyanthes trifoliata (bog bean)
Scirpus zebrinus (zebra rush)
Typha minima (reed mace)

Evergreens with glossy leaves
Ceanothus arboreus (vars)
Choisya ternata
Escallonia rubra/macanthra
Griselinia littoralis
LEFT Ilex (hollies, many)
Laurus nobilis (sweet bay)
Olearia x haastii
Mahonia (vars)

Arching, spraying, hanging forms
Garrya elliptica (grey catkins)
Corylus maxima
Cytisus (many brooms)
Genista lydia (and others)
Buddleia davidii
Viburnum plicatum
Philadelphus (vars)
Polygonatum (Solomon's Seal)
Dierama (Angels' fishing rods)
LEFT Artemisia 'Guizhou Group'

Ground covers of character
Pachysandra terminalis
Sarcococca humilis
Ajuga reptans (purple var.)
Vinca major/minor
Hederas (ivies)
Tiarella cordifolia
Alchemilla mollis
Viburnum davidii
Epimedium x rubrum
Bergenia cordifolia
Cornus canadensis
RIGHT Saxifraga x urbium (London Pride)

Spires, swords and fans
Iris (all)
Verbascum olympicum
Astilbes (all)
LEFT (D. x mertonensis) Digitalis (foxglove)
Yuccas (all)
Aruncus dioicus
Eremurus (all)
Rheum palmatum
Ligularia (all)
Phormium (all)
Ferns (most)

Exotic companions for house and terrace
Aralia
Agaves
Aloes
Cleome
Cordyline
Dracaena
Ficus (fig)
Monstera
Musa (banana)
Philodendron
Pittosporum
Tradescantia

Arne Jacobsen,
paving for a private garden

Mien Ruys,
'Roof' Garden and
Marsh Garden, Dedemsvaart

Mien Ruys,
detail from
the 'Roof' Garden,
Dedemsvaart

Concrete walkway
from *Pflanzen und Blumen*,
Stuttgart 1970

Paving display,
from *Pflanzen und Blumen*,
Stuttgart 1970

Mien Ruys,
the 'Roof' Garden,
Dedemsvaart

Frederick Gibberd,
pavings made *in situ*,
with cobbles in concrete,
Marsh Lane, Harlow

Circular concrete paviours,
on display at the Hamburg
Gartenschau, *c.* 1965

Dan Kiley,
Miller house,
Columbus, Indiana

133

OPPOSITE
From the main steps the view down the terraces is cleverly manipulated to appear as one great layout: the sphinx, the santolina patterns, the pool and the green parterre are on four descending levels.

LEFT
The villa entrance.

BELOW
The entire main vista from the lowest level of the terraces to the villa high above.

Page designed gardens on each side of the main vista. Neptune in his own pool (opposite) looks across the main terrace level to the steps (below) rising to the canal garden and his companionably baroque pineapples. (right) Neptune and other details, such as this seat, are harmoniously understated.

mien **ruys**

dedemsvaart, *netherlands*

Mien Ruys's gardens abound with amusing details that display her modern turn of mind.

TOP LEFT
Small scale sculptures arouse attention.

TOP RIGHT
'Functional' ornament.

BOTTOM LEFT
'Half-casks', painted white and arranged casually, contrast with a formal and expensively made seat.

BOTTOM RIGHT
An elevated circle among circles.

Wilhelmina 'Mien' Jacoba Ruys (1904–98) was born in Dedemsvaart, a small town in the Overijssel district of the mid-Netherlands, east of Zwolle. One of the chief features of the little town was her father's Royal Moerheim Nursery, where she grew up and took to gardening perfectly naturally. From the beginning everything Ruys was to do in what is now her own garden, seemed intuitively to reflect a prevailing mood in the modern garden story: her first garden, made when she was twenty-one, seems to echo the mood of pioneering German naturalism. In 1927–28 she made an excursion to England, working for a while with the contracting firm of Wallace and Sons in Tunbridge Wells (where George Dillistone was the chief designer) and meeting the aged Gertrude Jekyll at Munstead Wood. She returned to Moerheim to make 'her classic English border' in 1927, which still survives. Ruys continued her studies, at the Berlin-Dahlem botanic garden and at architectural school in Delft: she began to practice subsequently as a garden architect, progressing rapidly to large-scale landscape schemes, which occupied her professionally until she retired in her sixties. Although she liked to acknowledge the influence of Gertrude Jekyll and William Robinson on her planting design, their styles were overlaid with her instinctive empathy with the Dutch modernists. She met many of the modern architects and acknowledged Van Doesburg and Mondrian as particular influences (as well as Christopher Tunnard) and she worked with Jan Bijhouwer and other famous landscape architects throughout her career. All her work displays the assurance of modern design at its very best: a garden for a block of flats in Antwerp (1962) has a broad-hedged rectangle, enclosing seats and large squares of flowers, another in Amsterdam-Noord (1967) reveals a hint of Burle Marx with great clumps of purple and green foliage spreading out from random 'beds' where the pavings have been removed.

Ruys continued to make a series of twenty-five 'demonstration' gardens for the Moerheim Nursery, of which almost every one is a complete modern creation in its own right. Her critical eye and professional confidence maintained each garden with necessary renovation, in its essentially designed form and character – she had integrity enough to know that once a job had been done well there was no point in tampering with it.

LEFT
Many of the small gardens
are grouped around a large
lawn; this view looks north
across the lawn and the
Yellow Garden, based on a
simple circle of bricks, to
the Mixed Border (originally
made in 1974) in front of
the tall hedge.

BELOW
The Yellow Garden
(originally made in 1982),
the border against the fence
to the Marsh Garden.

Modern design can grow old gracefully. Here the use of concrete for pavings and pool construction has mellowed into its setting. In Mien Ruys' skilled hands even concrete can become romantic.

post-war europe:
a second flowering

The modern garden returned to post-war Europe in the hand-baggage of landscape architecture, as a kind of culture-supplement in the parcels of American aid to recovery. It was to be a device of re-unification (in that part of Europe then in the West) and of the reconstruction of bomb-shattered cities. Landscape architects were to provide the settings for new housing, hospitals and schools, and the workplace, whether factory or office complex, was to be in a garden.

Many aspects of the modern story, so drastically abbreviated by the war, were replayed: Corbusian tiers of flats would rise from natural gardens of asymmetrical planning, with rocks and watery groves of architectural planting: for families and retired couples there were to be houses with gardens, and design was to bless even the smallest plot.

Sylvia Crowe's *Garden Design,* published in 1958, was a complete textbook of history and design. The garden history section ended with 'The Contemporary Garden' to which the author assigned the following definition: 'The most recent of the long historic line of garden traditions which is now evolving in America began to emerge in Northern

A modern version of the traditional hornbeam allee, designed by Sylvia Crowe for a garden in Sussex in the 1960s. This garden, typical of many designed by the distinguished landscape architects Sylvia Crowe and Brenda Colvin, has been discreetly and loyally maintained by the original client for almost forty years. Many similar smaller modern gardens go unremarked on the housing market, and are thus destroyed through ignorance and changes in ownership.

Frederick Gibberd, Marsh Lane, Old Harlow, Essex. The tapestry hedge, a mid-twentieth century fashion.

and J. H. Shepherd studied the Italian villa gardens, Jellicoe admitted that they both 'felt the need of a realistic grounding in the classics before tackling the modern world which we knew to be upon us'.[3] Yet he was always ready to question that new world: during his time as studio master at the Architectural Association in the early 1930s he chose to interview five sculptors, whose work he admired but did not understand – Eric Gill, Frank Dobson, Elizabeth Muntz, Eric Kennington and Henry Moore. He also confessed a 'mystical attraction' to the sculptor Gaudier-Brzeska, and to being completely won over by Naum Gabo and *CIRCLE*. He claimed that the necessity of maintaining a private practice brought him clients who wanted 'new gardens in old settings'. The old settings were the precious private symbols of a lifestyle rooted in traditions (even if a renegade duke built a modern house he still crammed it with antiques, heraldic beasts and crested silver and stuffed the garden with baroque jardinières).

The British, however sleek and contemporary their factories or schools, clung on to their traditions at home, and this pervaded all classes. The secret of Jellicoe's success was that he understood just how much of the modern the British – singly or in groups – could take: his Church Hill Memorial garden at Walsall is one of his most subtle compromises.

Later in his life, Jellicoe became more emotionally involved with the whole world of modern art. He used to tell the story, as a tribute to his friend Frederick Gibberd, that when they were both designing new towns in 1947 (Gibberd designed Harlow, Jellicoe Hemel Hempstead) Jellicoe questioned Gibberd about the paintings on his wall – an unrelievedly modern collection. Gibberd replied, 'they flow electricity into me'. Jellicoe wrote 'I began to push wider open the door to the unknown of which I had had a glimpse... [Picasso came] like a thunderbolt from on high.' He made a small, talismanic collection of watercolours and sketches by Moore,

Nicholson, Sutherland, and Ivon Hitchens and others, which became the key to his late works.[4]

Frederick Gibberd (1908–84) was perhaps the most convinced and outwardly committed of British moderns. He threw all his characteristic talents, ambition and verve into his uncompromisingly modern buildings – the first buildings for Heathrow Airport, Didcot Power Station, the InterContinental Hotel at Hyde Park Corner and the Roman Catholic Cathedral in Liverpool (affectionately known as 'Paddy's Wigwam'). As a landscape architect he designed Kielder Reservoir in Northumberland, Europe's largest man-made lake, and the Stratford-upon-Avon riverside; as a town planner he laid out Harlow new town. Over twenty strenuous and busy years, from 1956, and into his retirement, he made his one and only garden, at the weekend bungalow which became his final home, at Marsh Lane, on the outskirts of Harlow. The site was 'a small farmery' of about six acres, on north-facing meadows sloping gently to a stream: a previous owner, with a stroke of naive genius, had planted an avenue of limes much too close together, and built a small concrete gazebo. Gibberd was pragmatic, no fair-weather gardener:

> in my climate, one has to accept that the form
> and colour of a design in summer fundamentally
> changes in winter. If someone tells me he is a keen
> gardener I ask to see his garden in February. Has it
> become a barren waste? Or does it still retain its
> form? Most English gardeners are horticulturists
> preoccupied with growing flowers. But garden
> design is concerned with colour in Spring, Summer,
> Autumn and Winter...

It was perhaps a necessary release that he was working in the large scale, on the plan for Harlow, walking the entire area, sensitive to the fall of the ground, at the same time: he was conscious of the same principles applied in each case, the garden was a miniature of the new town landscape, and received equal care, equal appreciation of form and natural features, in everything but scale:

To me landscape and garden design is like town design, an art of space. A series of rooms or spaces are made each with its own character... spaces merge imperceptibly into each other. Whichever of these spaces you choose to enter there will be others beyond them. The pattern is cellular. It is a garden to be explored, not led through.[5]

Frederick Gibberd, Marsh Lane, Old Harlow, Essex. A pot by Monica Young beneath an aged and gnarled quince tree.

Frederick Gibberd, M
Lane, Old Harlow, Es
The columns and urn
salvaged from the ne
classical facade of Co
Bank, the Strand, Lor
which he modernized

arne **jacobsen**

st catherine's, *oxford, uk*

Carl Theodor Sorensen's alter ego and sometime collaborator was the great architect Arne Jacobsen (1902–71), who brought Danish design to the wider world. Jacobsen studied at the Royal Academy of Fine Arts in the 1920s, and exhibited a student project, a chair, at the 1925 Paris exposition; his early architecture was seen as Corbusian, and was considered controversial. Jacobsen was yet another master of duality, who journeyed through much of the twentieth century combining modern theory with a particular native genius. He was also a gardener – and in many instances – including St Catherine's College, Oxford – he acted as his own landscape architect, the modern gardener par excellence. Jacobsen lived modestly in his own housing scheme at Klampenborg, Copenhagen, tending a collection of plants which inspired him, and which contributed to his designs for his wife's Jonna Moller's fabric printing.

It was Danish pre-eminence in architecture and design that attracted the attention of an Oxford University Committee that was seeking an architect for the new St Catherine's in 1958: the founding Master, the distinguished historian Alan Bullock, was determined to have a building that represented the best of its own time. A deputation inspected Jacobsen's Arhus University, the Munkegard School in Vangede, Rodovre town hall, and the architect's home and garden, and – even though it was a wintry tour – Jacobsen's genius for buildings which respond to their settings shone through, and he was offered the appointment. In turn, the architect visited Oxford, he studied the atmosphere of the ancient buildings of New College, and liked the site of Holywell Great Meadow. Eventually everyone involved was so optimistic that Jacobsen's commission was as he wished – for the entity of the buildings, gardens and fittings and furniture for the new college.

It was a remarkable achievement, and not all plain sailing by any means, but Oxford has in St Catherine's College the most complete demonstration of the tenets of modern living to be found in Britain, and possibly in Europe. The building and its garden embody almost everything this book has to say: towards the end of his life Jacobsen chose the college as his favourite among buildings he had designed.

The details of Jacobsen's composition allow a constant interplay between intimate corners and larger views. These are all general circulation areas between college buildings.

The canal and long lawn
extend along the front of the
college. Barbara Hepworth's
bronze *Archaean* is to the
right of the path to the
Porter's Lodge.

LEFT
Inside, the Quadrangle, with
its great circle of grass and
asymmetrical cedar, is the
hub of the college.

FOLLOWING PAGES
The planting, started in
1965, is rich in rare and
interesting specimens.
Though of an English
luxuriance rather greater
than Jacobsen imagined, it
displays restrained grace
and integrity.

Jacobsen's characteristic
free-standing wall and
hedge blocks give practical
shelter from rain and wind,
but in their differing lights
and seasons they invite a
lighthearted progress –
games of hide and seek –
expressing the exuberance
of youth with which the
garden has such empathy.

The modern garden:
to be continued?

The history of garden design is one of minorities, of a few exponents of a style who make a mark which has been handed down over the years: design traditions have come to us by courtesy of a comparatively few mogul potentates and renaissance princes, a bevy of Whig landlords, or more recently even one absurdly young architect allied to a middle-aged spinster artist-gardener. It was not surprising that the mystique of the modern garden should rest with a few landscape-architects and designers when it arrived in the sixth decade of the twentieth century.

The 1960s were dubbed a decade of 'tumult and change' on the cover of the special issue of *Life* magazine for 22 December 1969: it showed the faces of Kennedys, Martin Luther King, Marilyn Monroe, soldiers in Vietnam, the Beatles, Richard Nixon and a Man on the Moon. The decade seemed – perhaps to compensate for the tumult – to demand more than other decades, dealing in marching throngs, packing stadiums and topping charts: success was married to mass appeal and selling by the million, popularly symbolized by the Warhol image and the tasty reality of Campbell's Condensed Tomato Soup. If the modern garden was to survive it would have to find a mass

Arne Jacobsen,
St Catherine's College,
Oxford (see pp. 176–83).

popularity, it would have to become a packaged constituent of consumer heaven, rather in the way that Gropius and other pioneers had imagined it as part of the unitary package, thirty years before. It is worth assessing what that package might have contained, making some estimate of the riches that comprised, as Sylvia Crowe had said, 'a standard of attainable excellence for the small and modest garden'.

The modern garden was a design ethos for modern people, as ubiquitous as the motor car or washing machine, above nationalist sentiments and arbitrations of taste, and yet eminently adaptable to site, soil and climate, to financial means and variable commitments. It encouraged an intensely close relationship between the house and its site, whether the house was a translucent object, partly of glass, which allowed the rooms to go out to meet the garden, and the air and scents of flowers to flow through it, or whether it was more substantial and sculpted into the form of the ground as Mendelsohn and Chermayeff's Shrubswood. Of course, it could be both, like Mendelsohn's own beloved house 'am Rupenhorn'. The house could be set (regulations permitting) at any point on a long narrow site, making way for a kaleido-scopic progress through carefully balanced spaces, a Corbusian design for a garden: orchard, lawn, flowers and groves are juggled to give privacy from neighbours, to let in the sun or keep out the wind, and all explored via a weaving path of paviours set in grass, as shown by Caneel-Claes. What could be more satisfactory than flower and vegetable plots echoing the familiar basic proportions of the building blocks of childhood, what more amusing than to play geometrical games with boxes and chequers and flowers, or to join Sørensen's play on circles and spirals? For the garden wishing to enter the portals of art there was Mondrian's guidance, there were the dancing curves of Picasso and Arp, and the purposeful abstract arrangements of Klee, Kandinsky and Moholy-Nagy: Page relied upon what he could learn from the invisible connections of objects, a tree, a rock, the distant mountain in his view, constructing his garden in space and time. The smallest space, perhaps treated diagonally (and both Le Corbusier and Jacobsen enjoyed designing triangular corner plots) can be induced to wrap

about the shoulders as a private green room: the tiniest court can hold a brimming pool and giant rhubarb, can be a chequerboard of herbs or a planted pavement of thymes, gentians and *Viburnum davidii.*

The larger the garden the more free and natural it could become, and the modern garden was infinitely flexible so that the amount of labour was a matter of choice. Grass was treated as a river of green, flowing into groves and woods, kept as daisy-pied 'lawn' at Brenda Colvin's Little Peacocks and Frederick Gibberd's Marsh Lane, as a foil for plant textures and sculptures. But even grass could display seasonal talents, flower-strewn in spring with a narrow path cut through it, perhaps the 'cut' widened when late summer turned the seed heads to tawny gold. The modern garden was allowed to live, and die: the seed heads and falling leaves were allowed their own particular beauty and season. Within the bounds of this integrity – which was derived from the respect that modern artists, like Moore and Hepworth, had for their materials, delights materialized – grass steps, green terraces, Mien Ruys's sculptured lawns, tapestried hedges, Arne Jacobsen's immaculate blocks of hedging, half-built rooms which encourage hide-and-seek, and Pietro Porcinai's sweeping, scented hedges on a Tuscan hillside. Hedges, too, were newly respected:they were substantial, simply geometrical and more often freely blowing. Both Porcinai and Sylvia Crowe used contrasting bands of hedging, something low and free – lavender or rosemary – backed by a taller, dense evergreen, griselinia or holly, with a third and highest layer of further contrast. Water, naturally, was accorded equal respect: pools, from the smallest to one of Porcinai's sublime rectangles, were of simple outline, brimful and (sometimes) bubbling, the water allowed to tumble in falls and rills (but not to spout inelegantly). The modern designers put water plants very high in their affections, and they also seemed to adore stepping stones or slatted walks across water. Slats lead to deckings, a practical and beautiful way to leave the natural ground undisturbed, or simply out of sight: Mien Ruys, who was always sensitive to environmental issues, used recycled plastic and redundant railway sleepers in preference to tropical hardwoods in her garden, and the ethics of availability is important in the modern philosophy. Endless riches lay in the grasp of designers in the 1960s. The consumer revolution awaited the modern garden: the question is, what happened to it?

The answer comes swiftly: almost nothing. Doubts and defections from modern purity rumble almost throughout this tale. By 1960 the word 'modern' was outdated, almost thirty years old, and the pioneers were distinguished, elderly, and listened to out of politeness. Gropius, still teaching at the Harvard Graduate School of Design, never conceded the supremacy of the architect as master builder – an attitude in itself which was a barrier to the revision of the very recent past.[1] Architects in general ceased to be interested in gardens, leaving the territory to landscape architects as partners in the new scenario of the design team.

The fate of the modern garden was dictated by the retiring gentility that seems to be the nature of landscape architects: they were seldom flamboyant or publicity-minded, and they had a professional interest in keeping design theory as the prerogative of a few. In Britain the small profession was socially cohesive (both Sylvia Crowe and Brenda Colvin were the daughters of civil servants with knighthoods; Geoffrey Jellicoe and Frederick Gibberd fitted socially). Britain was still commonwealth-minded and led the thinking in the world that had been coloured pink on the map. European co-operation was fraught with language barriers and developing only in fits and starts; the healthy state of modern design in the hands of a Dutchwoman, Mien Ruys, or a Dane, Carl Theodor Sørensen, was confined to their own national boundaries. Their work was little known in America, where it might have had admiration and influence. There 'nationalism' was breaking out too, in that California (and the design school at Berkeley in particular) was absorbed by the ecology of its natural habitat dry garden, almost turning its back on America to gaze fondly on the Pacific rim. In the Midwest, the

Mien Ruys, pool in the Wild Shade Garden, originally designed in 1925, in her own garden at Dedemsvaart, Holland.

University of Illinois had remained a bastion of Beaux-Arts that modernism had not breached. Stanley White (1891–1970) who embodied landscape teaching there for half a century, was a polymath who believed in the poet-philosopher role of the designer, and that poetry and ecology were rightly equal and inseparable concerns. White had an empathetic understanding of the Midwest's Nordic romanticism, he knew Jensen and had worked briefly in the offices of Fletcher Steele and the Olmsted brothers, but his belief in the social and spiritual values of landscape design were those of Frederick Law Olmsted, whose reputation he began to revive.[2]

The Harvard graduate school remained the fount of design thinking, and there White's influence was perpetuated in the slight form of his one-time pupil, Hideo Sasaki (b. 1919), who had arrived there in 1950

and was to mastermind the education of generations of designers for the next twenty years.[3] Sasaki's life experience is interesting (the whole of the story of the modern garden could be written with post-Freudian emphasis on the inner landscapes of the practitioners) – and in itself is another explanation for the demise of the modern garden. Sasaki was of Californian-Japanese farming stock, with an interest in the arts and a determination to escape from agriculture: he progressed through business administration and city planning only to be interned as an alien in the early 1940s, volunteering as a farm labourer to gain release. This brought him to Chicago, the city's legacy of Olmsted parks, and to Stanley White at the University of Illinois. White was extremely pessimistic about the state of his profession, which he felt 'may have its back against the

Dan Kiley, the Kimmel residence, Salisbury, Connecticut, 1996.

wall' in a battle against the iniquities of surveyors and engineers (this was Olmsted's, and Repton's, dying opinion, and has become a permanent professional neurosis).[4] Sasaki was to do more to refute this than anyone while he was at Harvard, forestalling the worst of the inter-disciplinary arguments by constructing the professional design team – assuming the role of manager, co-ordinator and critic which he carried into his own practice and the founding of the 'corporate office'.[5] Clearly a design team and a corporate office needed large commissions, and that was where the future lay: it seems rather petty to regret that Sasaki's nature was one of reserve and inward concentration, upon his students and his practice, that he disliked publicity and was not interested in plants – this last the legacy of his bad memories of farming. In any estimation he was a great teacher and a saviour of the landscape design profession, but the fate of the modern garden was irrelevant in his way of thinking.

The resurrection of Frederick Law Olmsted, the patron saint of the American landscape profession, finally drew back the heavy curtain that had dropped in the 1920s, hiding the past and isolating the modern belief in the present. Through Laura Wood Roper's masterly biography (1973) and the accompanying series of volumes of Olmsted's papers from the Library of Congress, Americans learned of their own historic landscape traditions.[6] Hundreds of nineteenth- and early twentieth-century parks and gardens created by Olmsted's firm all across America were identified and celebrated, inciting an interest in the whole sphere of garden history from the earliest colonial settlements to fabulous designs by Florence Yoch for Hollywood moguls and their film sets.[7] In Britain the founding of the Garden History Society in 1965 also unlatched the floodgates of the past: in a parallel to Olmsted, on a smaller scale, the resurrection of interest in Gertrude Jekyll (1843–1932) revealed dozens of her gardens, and those of Edwin Lutyens (1869–1942) surviving in all their stone-girt certainty and formality. Jekyll's writings on her favourite herbaceous perennials and scented-leaved shrubs were all reissued to inspire fresh interpretations of her multitudinous imagination; her German counterpart,

the nurseryman Karl Foerster (1874–1970) had an equivalent influence.[8] These were revivals to delight the nursery and horticultural industries, for they marked the return of an abundance, a 'jungle' of plants to fashion.

The horticultural industry in Britain and continental Europe also played a part in the downfall of the modern garden, largely because no one evaluated the possibilities of modern planting design, of designers' plants for temperate climates, in the way that Roberto Burle Marx did for the tropics. Russell Page's vain plea for hostas by the thousand for the 1951 Festival of Britain gardens at Battersea to an industry that could only supply a few hundred went unheeded: nurserymen and plantswomen struggling for post-war survival saw salvation in the provision of the greatest variety to the greatest number, encouraged by the introduction of container-grown plants in the mid-1960s. People who said they loved plants invariably sold them, and there was a culture of inclusivity with the emphasis on toughness and eye appeal: heathers, large-trumpeted narcissus, big-headed roses, and gold-leaved variegations of almost every evergreen shrub, rather than a concentration upon the essential quality of a species or cultivar. The modern taste for one or three plants of elegant form rather than a tangled mass of distortions, was viewed with hostility by the trade: many horticulturists have become entrenched in their opinion that any restraint or stringent judgment in the use of plants by landscape architects or designers, brands these moderns as plant haters. The pity is that, had anyone seriously analysed the plant qualities and characterizations of modern planting (described in chapter 4), they would have found that William Robinson, Henri Correvon, Gertrude Jekyll, Christopher Tunnard, James Rose and Mien Ruys all knew a good plant when they saw one, and it was often the same plant: it was not without irony that the Jekyll revival of one of her supreme favourites, the hosta, meant that the thousands of plants that Russell Page had wanted in 1951 were easily acquired for gardens of the 1980s.

The modern garden was to be smothered out of existence by jungles of perennials and old roses, and firmly rejected in favour of eclectic revivals of ornaments and features: the styles that Le Corbusier and Christopher Tunnard had so despised returned invigorated, all at once and usually all together in the same garden.[9] This consumerist avalanche was entirely beyond the control of the designers of the later twentieth century, who would not have wished to have anything to do with populist tastes anyway. For the final irony of the modern garden was that as a democratic notion – as the means of achieving the highest standards of design in small and medium-sized gardens, as Sylvia Crowe had advocated – it was rejected, with hardly any marketing, and little or no understanding. This rejection meant that the best professional designers were corralled with rich or corporate clients and large-scale projects, where they had traditionally been, rather than moving out into the socially responsible milieu that Garrett Eckbo and others had dreamed of. The modern garden was, or could have been, in Henry Moore's words, 'an expression of the significance of life… a stimulation to a greater effort in living'. Instead we have opted for the merely decorative, a materialistic mayhem, the dreadful and unnatural school of 'exterior decorating'.[10]

The profession of landscape architecture, at least in my knowledge of its practice in Britain, Europe and America, seems to have carelessly discarded a treasure in its neglect of the modern garden legacy. In Britain, Sir Geoffrey Jellicoe was unique in maintaining a large number of gardens (notably Shute House, Wiltshire, and Sutton Place, Surrey) amongst his landscape commissions.[11] He accomplished a creative compromise with many of his clients in the modern content of their design, which he sometimes controversially masked with his own interpretations of the client's subconscious wishes. This role, of the designer as psychic counsellor, was not in the professional syllabus, and for a land-based profession it was unpalatable: rather than lack of opportunity or insufficient fees, this was the underlying reason that landscape architects gave up private gardens. In doing so they gave up the popular constituency of their work, which has been reflected in their isolationist image. The newly formed profession of garden designers stepped into the breach from about the mid-1970s – extremely well versed in planting

techniques and hard landscaping, in client-friendly procedures and contract management, but less so in the history of design: to many garden designers the modern garden is a hazy notion from a distant past.

Russell Page (1906–85), though an early member of the Institute of Landscape Architects, has been the most distinguished designer to work outside the landscape profession. In his candid autobiography *The Education of a Gardener* (1962) he explained his solitary journey to find his own identity as a designer, equipped with little from his Lincolnshire upbringing but a love of plants and a short spell at the Slade School of Art in London. He sought out modern artists, found a sympathy with abstract art and an admiration for Burle Marx's 'vegetable abstractions by a kind of painting made with the heavy texture of tropical succulents'.[12] Page had a sentience for all experiences, he was by instinct and timing a modern believer – 'So-called abstract art', he wrote, makes 'a new impact on a part of consciousness not trained, or at least accustomed, to perceive classical art forms'.[13] But then, learning in reverse, he discovered classical art, and most importantly French formalism and the gardens of Le Nôtre through his friendship with André de Vilmorin, of the famous family of nurserymen in Paris, whose forebears had held royal appointments in the eighteenth century. Page found his spiritual home in France; his many commissions were to be in Europe, North and South America, and very few in Britain. His skills were in finding rich and aristocratic clients, and realizing – as he had as early as 1935 when working with Jellicoe for the Marquess of Bath – that such clients might like their avant-garde tastes to be acknowledged, but in their ancestral gardens, they favoured tradition. Page's brilliance was to balance tradition with a witty and astringent modern touch, as at his famous garden for Villa Silvio Pellico, outside Turin (see pp 136–41). Page's alter ego, the American designer and landscape gardener Lanning Roper (1912–83), who worked mostly in England and only on a few gardens in Europe and America, accomplished a similar balancing act throughout his career.

Page was the pivotal figure in the decline of the modern garden. He was such a wizard at negating its beliefs, at using expensive stone as if it were concrete, at returning the status of the garden to the aristocracy and ultra-rich, at designing breathtakingly simple pools, then mischievously adding a Reptonian rustic pavilion or some Louis quinze treillage, and at planting a grove of minimalist simplicity, then imprisoning it in axial symmetry. He can only be called a postmodernist. Where he led, so many of the designers practising today have followed, attributing an eclectic band of loyalties to strands of the past, whilst achieving that polished perfection of geometry and form that Page pioneered. This polished perfection has also been strongly influenced by the maintenance standards of the National Trust, particularly in the two gardens of mythological status to twentieth-century designers, Sissinghurst Castle in Kent and Hidcote Manor garden in Gloucestershire.

Today's influences constitute a world of extremes. Far out is the eccentric, expressionist Ian Hamilton Finlay's Little Sparta, his partly tended, partly wild Lanarkshire hillside dominated by rough weather, into which he has inserted sculptures, mottoes and messages. The messages, exquisitely carved in stone or wood, celebrate metaphor, they evoke comparisons between unlikely opposites, such as the 'charming place' image of a garden and the violence of the Second World War. Hamilton Finlay is an artist, and with other land artists, Andy Goldsworthy, Richard Long and Chris Drury, who celebrate a fellowship of elements and materials – piles of pebbles, swirls of stones, leaf-spattered pools – forms a legitimate source of inspiration for gardens. The distinguished Belgian designer Jacques Wirtz shrugs off the epithet 'the André Le Nôtre of the twentieth century' and culls his inspiration from music, memory and the work of the nineteenth-century Flemish artist Henri de Braekeleer.[14] The Wirtz trio of father and sons Martin and Peter are the grand masters of Europe, designing and restoring great avenues, planting curvilinear hedges and miscanthus groves but equally

Fernando Caruncho uses Spanish traditions in a modern context for his gardens.

happy with an ivy-floored glade or drift of Iceland poppies. The Spaniard Fernando Caruncho admires Russell Page, but hates Rousseau-romanticism and English garden nostalgia, finding his inspiration in the fabulous garden traditions of Spain.[15] The Dutchman Lodewijk Baljon enjoys the views from his canalside studio in Amsterdam, respects the Dutch water engineers who reclaimed his homeland and also Dutch modernism – he says 'Innovation in the art of garden design is not achieved through a radical rejection of the past… tradition gives us something to work with, a body of knowledge, but it is also something we can criticize and change.'[16] Ludwig Gerns has done just this in Hanover (see pp. 200–8), to show how the French modernists and the influence of Roberto Burle Marx live on.

In America the notable designers James van Sweden and Wolfgang Oehme have impeccable modern backgrounds in Holland and Germany: they became celebrated for bringing the grasses and flowers of steppe, sand dune and marsh into the climatically stressed urban malls of Washington, D.C., and they have adapted this eminently satisfying range of plants into delicately pretty wild gardens along the eastern shoreline, as well as sophisticated Georgetown gardens. Their point of reference, 'an American meadow, a place of freedom and ease where wildlife, plant life and human life co-exist in harmony', echoes Jens Jensen.[17] The dynamic Martha Schwartz, an artist with a background in theatre design, plunders other American icons for her vivacious designs – her Bagel garden in Boston is hedged in 16-inch high box, with purple gravel and precisely set out weatherproof bagel rolls alternating with purple ageratum set in brown soil. Martha Schwartz works at both landscape and garden scale (and to admit there is a difference is important): like Geoffrey Jellicoe, she likes to target the personal subconscious. In the summer of 1995 she was starting work on a third of an acre on the New Jersey shore when her client's son announced he was getting married. A marriage garden was arranged – bride and groom both being gardeners – with an avenue of handsome potted trees leading to the wedding tent, which was set in a field of empty, blue-painted flower pots. In the tent were black-eyed Susans (orange daisies)

and candles, and the wedding feast was taken in a sunflower grove, a grid of potted sunflowers on purple grass, with white-clothed tables set out in lines, Brueghel fashion, and orange trees.[18]

This catalogue of riches can go on and on, but takes us far from the modern garden. Back at Harvard, the erstwhile professor of landscape, Michael van Valkenburgh, has been reviving the philosophic notion of the American garden for student projects, and designing some 'private landscapes' himself: his Chestnut Hill birch garden is essentially a flight of wooden stairs, suggesting the rickety steps of Martha's Vineyard harboursides, where he spends his summers, down a slope thickly planted with evergreens and multi-stemmed birches, in a 'deliberate quotation' from Fletcher Steele's Naumkeag.[19]

We seem to have come full circle. Could it be possible that the rampant eclecticism of the recent years is beginning to pall? In another of his gardens Van Valkenburgh 'subscribes to the aesthetic principle that new materials and the latest technology dictate new forms'.[20] Does this not sound familiar? In Japan, Shodo Suzuki has retained the connection between modern art and science in his adoption of 'forms based on the fundamental principles of the physical world – including those from the macro- and micro-views'.[21] In 1956 Gyorgy Kepes edited a book with contributions from, among others, Jean Arp, Naum Gabo, Siegfried Giedion, Walter Gropius on exactly this subject, lavishly illustrated from scientific sources, especially the Massachusetts Institute of Technology.[22]

As we slip the bonds of the old millennium and of a century that has been obsessed with nostalgia for the past, is it possible that we can rediscover a belief in the present? Have we the courage to live with gardens and groves that honour our relationship with planet Earth, in mathematical and scientific analogy, in ecological richness and minimalist serenity? If so, then we will have found a common bond with most of the people in this book. Gardens are notoriously laggard, trailing in the wake of architecture and fashions in clothes and interiors: perhaps the exciting beginnings of seventy years ago were premature: perhaps the day of the modern garden is yet to come.

Garden for Mr and Mrs Ulrich Meyer on the southeastern shore of Lake Michigan, by Wolfgang Oehme and James van Sweden. The pines and dune grasses of the lake shore have prompted a beautiful and practical mix of ornamental grasses, sedum, yarrows, black-eyed Susan and Russian sage to blow beside the boardwalks and paths of this holiday garden.

luis **barragán**

mexico

'In the creation of a garden, the architect invites the partnership of the Kingdom of Nature. In a beautiful garden the majesty of nature is ever present, but it is nature reduced to human proportions and thus transformed into the most efficient haven against the aggressiveness of contemporary life.' Spoken in his native tongue, the words of 'the son of Mexico' on receiving the Pritzker Architecture Prize at Dumbarton Oaks in 1980, are Barragán's blessing on the modern garden. Barragán was born in 1902 in Guadalajara, brought up in the Mexican countryside, trained as an engineer and an architect, but believed himself to be a landscape architect, in the simplest conjunction of those two words. He stands at the point where architecture, gardens and sculpture meet and mingle, and in his lifelong preoccupation with the 'humanistic ecology' of his native land he refined a philosophy of universal relevance.

In his poor country Barragán had to struggle to make a living from design: he was first inspired by a visit to the 1925 Paris exposition, to the Mediterranean garden of the French poet and novelist Ferdinand Bac, and to the Alhambra at Granada. He felt that a private garden was an unknown notion in Mexican life, where leisure was taken in public places: his first major gardens introduced both public and private spaces into residential development at El Pedregal (1945–50), a volcanic landscape of fantastic rock formations and secret green valleys south of Mexico City. Walls, fountains and lawns were inserted into the dramatic natural setting 'to display the expressive and poetic potential of the land and the quality of life that could be created there'. This was Barragán's essential mission, and all his subsequent houses have private courtyards where serenity is induced by his sublime sculptural interplay of colour, proportion and the elegant pose of a single jacaranda tree or bush of myrtle. Plants, of minimalist practicability in arid settings, find fellowship with the occult symbolism of Japan in Barragán's courts.

Barragán's work was only revealed to the wider world by an exhibition at the Museum of Modern Art in New York in 1976; his Francisco Gilardi house in Mexico City was completed that year, a sculptural entity of inside and outside spaces, an internal pool and vividly coloured walls, all at play around the single jacaranda tree. This was his last completed work, and after ill health forced his retirement, he died in 1988 at his house in Tacubaya, Mexico City.

TOP RIGHT AND BOTTOM LEFT
The fountain bringing the water of life for man and horse into the court of the San Cristobal Stables (1967–68).

TOP LEFT AND BOTTOM RIGHT
Courtyard details of Barragán's own house and studio in Mexico City.

the modern garden

San Cristobal Stables: the sculpturally engineered fountain, bringing fresh water to the pool where the horses drink and bathe. One of several water courts designed by Barragán, it is both sculpture and garden; the Alhambra, Mies van der Rohe and Mondrian are all present in the inspiration.

luis **barragán**

OPPOSITE AND BELOW
The hitching rails, with
tree shade, and (below)
framed views, all parts of
the essential design.

LEFT AND FAR LEFT
The Drinking Trough
Fountain, set among the
shade of olive and
jacaranda groves.

OPPOSITE
Dappled shade and sunlight
add to the variety of shapes
and textures

LEFT
Restraint in the variety
of plants enhances the
contrasts.

BELOW
Sculptural plants, including
a 'cloud-pruned' yew at the
corner of the villa.

FOLLOWING PAGES
Magical effects of
immaculately cut pavings
and wedges and mounds
of planting that dance and
swirl across the lawns.

Balance and contrast
created by the massings of
flowers and hedges, open
spaces, and mature trees.

FOLLOWING PAGE
A rare touch of symmetry.

notes

introduction

1   Alma (formerly Mahler) Gropius left him for the Expressionist writer and architect Franz Werfel, taking their children, three-year-old Marion and baby son Martin (d. May 1919) with her. See Reginald Isaacs's biography, *Gropius*, 2 vols. 1983–84, English language ed. Little Brown, New York, 1991.

2   Isaacs, *Gropius*, p. 62.

3   Naum Gabo (Noton Pevsner), *The Realistic Manifesto*, Moscow 1920, from *Naum Gabo 1890–1977 Centenary Exhibition* catalogue, Annela Juda Fine Art, London 1990.

4   Arnold Whittick, *Eric Mendelsohn: A Life*, Leonard Hill Ltd, London 1956, p. 47.

5   Walter Segal, Banister Fletcher Professor, University College London, lecture to School of Environmental Studies 1973, published in *Architectural Review*, January 1974, pp. 31–38. Too young for the war, Segal was brought up close to Henri Oedenkoven's radical Ascona community (which spawned both Lenin and Walt Disney).

6   Albert Christ-Janer, *Eliel Saarinen*, University of Chicago Press, 1948, 1979 ed., pp. 9–26.

7   Reyner Banham, *Guide to Modern Architecture*, Architectural Press, London 1962, p. 16.

8   Walter Gropius, memorandum to the AEG, March 1910, 'Programme for the Establishment of a Company for the Provision of Housing on Aesthetically Consistent Principles', published in *Architectural Review*, July 1961, pp. 49–51.

9   From the text by Sigrid Achenbach to the exhibition catalogue of his architectural drawings from the Kunstbibliothek, Berlin at the Cooper-Hewitt Museum, New York, 1988–89, trans. John Gabriel, ed. Karen Margolis.

10 Geoffrey Jellicoe, '"Soundings, Decade 1960–1970", The Underworld of Art', in *The Studies of a Landscape Designer over Eighty Years*, vol. 1, Garden Art Press, 1993, p. 40–41.

11 Siegfried Giedion, *Space, Time and Architecture: the Growth of a New Tradition*, Harvard University Press, Cambridge, MA, 1959 (3rd ed.), p. 396.

12 Anne Whiston Spirn, 'Frank Lloyd Wright, Architect of Landscape', in David G. De Long (ed.), *Frank Lloyd Wright, Designs for an American Landscape 1922–1932*, Thames and Hudson, London 1996, p. 155.

13 'The Japanese Print: An Interpretation' (1912) is in Wright's *Collected Writings*, vol. II (1930–32), ed. Bruce Brooks Pfeiffer, New York, Rizzoli/FLW Foundation, 1992. See also Spirn's essay, as in note 12 above, pp. 135–59.

14 Edward Wiebe, *The Paradise of Childhood, a practical guide to Kindergarteners* (including the life and work of Friedrich Froebel), Milton Bradley Company, Washington, 1896.

15 Robert McCarter, *Frank Lloyd Wright*, Phaidon, London 1997, p. 40.

16 McCarter, *Frank Lloyd Wright*, p. 119.

17 Spirn, 'Frank Lloyd Wright, Architect of Landscape', p. 156.

18 *Ibid.*

19 *Ibid.*, p. 157.

chapter**one**

1   Paul Overy, *De Stijl*, Thames and Hudson, London 1991 (1997 ed.), p. 91.

2   Overy, *De Stijl*, p. 72.

3   Antony Kok, one of the signatories of the 1918 De Stijl manifesto, 'was a gardening expert' (Overy, *De Stijl*, p. 92). See also Allen Doig, *Theo van Doesburg, Painting into Architecture, Theory into Practice*, Cambridge 1986.

4   Doig, *Theo van Doesburg*, p. 67

5   See Jurgen Joedicke, *Weissenhofsiedlung Stuttgart*, Karl Kramer Verlag, Stuttgart, 1990.

6   Overy, *De Stijl*, p. 113.

7   Michel Seuphor, *Mondrian*, Abrams, New York, n.d. (*c.* 1960), pp. 303–7.

8   Dorothée Imbert, *The Modernist Garden in France*, Yale University Press, 1993, p. 148.

9   Le Corbusier, *Towards a New Architecture*, trans. Frederick Etchells, Architectural Press 1927, 1978 ed., pp. 216–17.

10 'Although Le Corbusier's architecture and urbanism have been studied, analyzed, and continuously re-evaluated… his approach to landscape design remains largely unscrutinized' (Imbert, *The Modernist Garden in France*, p. 147). Compare an editorial by Peter Davey to the gardens edition of the *Architectural Review*, September 1989: 'One of the great failings of the High Modern Movement was that it valued gardens so little. Not only were private gardens often excluded from housing layouts, but the Movement failed to produce a body of theory and practice of gardens…'

11 Imbert, *The Modernist Garden in France*, p. 156.

12 See Tim Benton, *The Villas of Le Corbusier 1920–30*, Yale University Press, 1987, p. 174. Le Corbusier's work with Crepin is well documented in the Fondation Le Corbusier archive.

13 Benton, *The Villas of Le Corbusier 1920–30*, p. 95. Benton's fascinating coverage of the drawings for this project also shows a photograph of the garden in existence.

14 Imbert, *The Modernist Garden in France*, p. 168.

15 Both Benton (pp. 209–17) and Imbert (pp. 167–73) treat 'the cosmopolitan millionaire' (Benton, p. 209) Charles de Beistegui's roof garden in detail, illustrating the lavish garden ideas evident in the drawings in FLC archive.

16 Benton quotes the dedication in a copy of *Oeuvre Complète II* sent to M. Touhladjian, Mayor of Poissy, 15 July 1960: 'Here then is the villa, born in 1929. It was happy in its limpid clarity. So was I.' (*The Villas of Le Corbusier 1920–30*, p. 191)

17 Benton, *The Villas of Le Corbusier 1920–30*, p. 195, quoting *Oeuvre Complète II*, p. 24.

18 Quoted in Imbert, *The Modernist Garden in France*, p. 166.

19 Quoted in Whittick, *Eric Mendelsohn: A Life*, p. 42.

20 *Ibid.*, p. 60.

21 Patrick Trevor-Roper, *The World Through Blunted Sight, An inquiry into the influence of defective vision on art and character*, 1970, rev. ed. Viking 1988, p. 120.

22 Quoted in Whittick, *Eric Mendelsohn: A Life*, p. 114.

23 Peter Blundell Jones, 'Towards a formal analysis of Mendelsohn's work', in *Erich Mendelsohn 1887–1953*, catalogue of *Modern British Architecture* (touring exhibition), 1987 (1997 ed. Friends of the De La Warr Pavilion, Bexhill-on-Sea, East Sussex), p. 15.

24 Letter from Argentinian journalist Victoria Ocampo to Erich Mendelsohn, *c.* 1930. From Oscar Beyer (ed.), *Letters of an Architect*, trans. Geoffrey Strachan, Abelard-Schuman 1967, pp. 109–10.

25 Erich Mendelsohn, letters dated 23 April 1942 and 10 July 1945. From Beyer (ed.), *Letters of an Architect*, pp. 156–57.

26 Douglas Cooper, 'Paul Klee' in *The Penguin Modern Painters*, 1949, p. 10–11, from the text of 'Über die moderne Kunst', a lecture given by Paul Klee in 1924, published in Berne 1945, pp. 11–14.

27 Georg Schmidt quoted in Cooper, 'Paul Klee'. See also Robert Melville's discussion of Klee's 'Architectural Mirages', *Architectural Review*, September 1956, 145–49.

masterworkone
fletcher **steele**

1 Fletcher Steele, 'Modern Landscape Architecture', *Contemporary Landscape Architecture and its Sources* (exhibition catalogue), San Francisco Museum, 1937, p. 23.

2 *Ibid.*, p. 25.

3 Mac Griswold and Eleanor Weller, *The Golden Age of American Gardens: Proud Owners, Private Estates 1890–1940,* Abrams/Garden Club of America, 1991, p. 58.

4 *Ibid.*, p. 59, quoting letter from Fletcher Steele to Esther Steele, 25 September 1950, Rochester Historical Society, New York.

masterworktwo
gabriel **guevrekian**

1 Elisabeth Viton et al., *Gabriel Guevrekian, 1900–1970: une autre architecture moderne*, Connivances, Paris 1987.

chaptertwo

1 See David Elliott, 'Gropius in England: A Documentation 1934–37', dedicated to the memory of Jack and Molly Pritchard, in Charlotte Benton, *A Different World: Emigré Architects in Britain 1928–1958*, RIBA Heinz Gallery, London, 1995.

2 See Reginald Snell, *From the Bare Stem: Making Dorothy Elmhirst's Garden at Dartington Hall*, Devon Books, 1989. See also my biography *Beatrix, The Gardening Life of Beatrix Jones Farrand 1872–1959*, Viking, New York, 1995. Michael Young suggests that the Elmhirsts did not take to Gropius, though they did give the money to support Gropius and Fry's design fees for Impington College, Cambridgeshire (*The Elmhirsts of Dartington*, Routledge & Kegan Paul, 1982, p. 229).

3 Charlotte Johnson, unpublished thesis on Percy Cane for the Architectural Association Garden Conservation Diploma Course, London, 1998.

4 Graham Thurgood, 'Silver End Garden Village 1926–1932', *The Thirties Society Journal No. 3 for 1982*, 1983, pp. 36–40.

5 J. L. Martin, 'The State of Transition', in *CIRCLE*, Faber & Faber 1937, p. 215.

6 Martin, 'The State of Transition', p. 216

7 *Ibid.*

8 *Ibid.*, p. 215

9 Christopher Hussey, on Joldwynds, *Country Life*, 15 September 1934, p. 281.

10 See Christine Boydell, *The Architect of Floors: modernism, art and Marion Dorn designs*, Schoeser in association with the British Architectural Library, RIBA, London, 1996.

11 Roy Strong, *Royal Gardens*, 1992, p. 144. See also Michael Spens, *The Complete Landscape Designs and Gardens of Geoffrey Jellicoe*, Thames and Hudson, London 1994, p. 52–53.

12 Barbara Tilson, 'Serge Chermayeff and the Mendelsohn Chermayeff partnership', in *Erich Mendelsohn 1887–1953* (exhibition catalogue), 1997 ed., pp. 59–67.

13 Jeremy Brook, quoting *The Times* architectural correspondent, in 'The story of the De La Warr Pavilion', *Erich Mendelsohn 1887–1953* (exhibition catalogue), 1997, p. 31.

14 Mendelsohn wrote continually in these terms: the 'naked babe' was the Weizman house, the planting plan for the Haifa hospital 'was filled' in a letter 8 September 1937; on 2 May 1938 he wrote with delight of the 'fuller, brighter and more alive' Schocken house garden, and the 'good green Lord' comes in a letter written on the Day of Atonement, 6 October 1938. All letters from Jerusalem, in Oscar Beyer (ed.), *Letters of an Architect*, trans. Geoffrey Strachan, Abelard-Schuman 1967, pp. 153–55.

15 Barbara Tilson, 'The Battle of Bentley Wood', in *The Thirties Society Journal no. 5*, 1985, pp. 24–31.

16 Roger Berthoud, *Life of Henry Moore*, 1987, p. 156.

17 Naum Gabo, 'Constructive art', *The Listener*, vol. xvi no. 408, 4 November 1936, reprinted in Jeremy Lewison (ed.), *Circle: Constructive art in Britain 1934–40*, Kettle's Yard Gallery, Cambridge, 1982, pp. 59–61.

18 Frances Spalding, *British Art Since 1900*, Thames and Hudson, London, 1986, p. 107.

19 Quoted by Rupert Martin, 'Moore in Landscape,' *Landscape,* September 1988.

20 Barbara Hepworth, in *CIRCLE*, p. 115.

21 Christopher Neve, *Unquiet Landscape: Places and Ideas in 20th century English Painting*, Faber 1990, p. 126.

22 *Ibid.*, p. ix.

23 Herbert Read, 'Ben Nicholson and the future of painting', *The Listener*, 9 October 1935, reprinted in Jeremy Lewison (ed.), *Circle: Constructive art in Britain 1934–40*, Kettle's Yard Gallery, Cambridge, 1982, pp. 62–63.

24 Neve, *Unquiet Landscape*, p. 127.

25 *Ibid.*, p. 129.

26 *Ibid.*, p. ix.

27 Barbara Hepworth, *A Pictorial Autobiography*, Tate Gallery, London, 1985, p. 9.

28 Hepworth, in *CIRCLE*, p. 113.

29 Moore, in *CIRCLE*, p. 118.

30 Moore, 'The Sculptor Speaks', *The Listener*, August 1937, reprinted in *Circle: Constructive art in Britain 1934–40*, 1982, p. 67–68.

31 *Ibid.*

32 Alan Powers, 'A Zebra at Villa Savoye': in *The Modern House Revisited*, 1996, p. 23.

33 Neve, *Unquiet Landscape*, p. 3

34 *Ibid*.

35 Neil Bingham, *Christopher Nicholson, RIBA Drawings Monograph no. 4*, Academy Editions, 1996, pp. 15–16.

36 'Flying, especially gliding, was as important as architecture' – for a brilliant elaboration of this see Bingham, *Christopher Nicholson*, pp. 18–19, which includes a list of the bombers and fighters Nicholson flew during the Second World War – the aeroplanes 'were like flying works of architecture for Nicholson'. He died whilst competing as a member of the British team in the International Gliding Championships in Switzerland in 1948.

37 Bingham, *Christopher Nicholson*, p. 17.

38 Lance M. Neckar, 'Christopher Tunnard: The Garden in the Modern Landscape', in Marc Treib (ed.), *Modern Landscape Architecture: A Critical Review*, MIT Press, 1993, p. 145. See also my correspondence with Tunnard's relatives, and essay, 'Christopher Tunnard', *Eminent Gardeners*, 1990, pp. 115–38.

39 Reyner Banham, 'Ornament and Crime: The Decisive Contribution of Adolf Loos', *The Architectural Review*, February 1957, pp. 85–88.

40 Todd and Mortimer, *The New Interior Decoration*, introduction, quoted in *Eminent Gardeners*, p. 126.

plans **analysis**

1 See Jeremy Gould, 'Gazetteer of Modern Houses in the United Kingdom and Republic of Ireland', in *The Modern House Revisited, Twentieth Century Architecture 2*, The Twentieth Century Society, London, 1996.

2 See 'The Rise of the Small Garden' in my *The Pursuit of Paradise, A Social History of Gardens and Gardening*, HarperCollins, 1999.

3 F. R. S. Yorke, *The Modern House in England*, Architectural Press 1937, pp. 49–52.

4   Michael Spens, *The Complete Landscape Designs and Gardens of Geoffrey Jellicoe*, Thames and Hudson, London, 1994, pp. 58–59.

5   Yorke, *The Modern House in England*, pp. 27–30 ('Group of Houses at Tewin, Herts, 1936'), and pp. 85–88 ('House at Bromley 1935').

chapterthree

1   Sarah P. Harkness, 'A New Way of Thinking' in 'Remembering Gropius', *Harvard University Graduate School of Design News*, Summer 1994, p. 20.

2   Franz Schulze, 'The Bauhaus Architects and the Rise of Modernism in the United States', in Stephanie Barron (ed.), *Exiles + Emigres: The Flight of European Artists from Hitler*, Los Angeles County Museum of Art/Abrams, 1997, pp 225–26.

3   *Long Island Modern: The First Generation of Modernist Architecture on Long Island, 1925–1960*, Guest Curator Alastair Gordon, exhibition Guild Hall Museum, East Hampton, New York, 1988.

4   Schulze, 'The Bauhaus Architects', p. 227.

5   Peter Walker and Melanie Simo, *Invisible Gardens: The Search for Modernism in the American Landscape*, MIT Press, 1994, p. 123.

6   James Rose, 'Freedom in the Garden', from *Pencil Points*, October 1938, reprinted in Treib (ed.), *Modern Landscape Architecture*, pp. 68–69.

7   For an outline of Tunnard's later career see my essay in *Eminent Gardeners*, 1990, and also Lance M. Neckar on Tunnard in Treib (ed.), *Modern Landscape Architecture*.

8   Tunnard's 'Modern Gardens for Modern Houses' (1942) is reprinted in Treib (ed.), *Modern Landscape Architecture*, pp. 159–65.

9   Tunnard, *Gardens in the Modern Landscape*, 1938 (1948 ed.), pp. 168–69.

10 Peter Shepheard, *Modern Gardens*, Architectural Press 1953, pp. 80–81.

11 Tunnard, 'Modern Gardens for Modern Houses', 1942, p.165.

12 Joseph Hudnut, 'The Modern Garden', in Tunnard, *Gardens in the Modern Landscape*, pp. 175–78.

13 Garrett Eckbo, 'Pilgrim's Progress', in Treib (ed.), *Modern Landscape Architecture*, p. 206.

14 Walker and Simo, *Invisible Gardens*, p. 123.

15 Eckbo, 'Pilgrim's Progress', p. 208–9.

16 Garrett Eckbo, 'The basic aim should be recreation', in F. A. Mercer (ed.), *The Studio Gardens and Gardening*, The Studio, London and New York, 1939, pp 18–20.

17 *Ibid.*, pp. 19–20.

18 Eckbo, 'Pilgrims' Progress', p. 210.

19 Eckbo, Kiley and Rose, 'Design for the urban environment', 1939, reprinted in Treib (ed.), *Modern Landscape Architecture*, p. 82.

20 Michael Laurie, *An Introduction to Landscape Architecture*, American Elsevier, 1975 (1976 ed.), p. 45.

21 Laurie, *An Introduction to Landscape Architecture*, p. 46.

22 Michael Laurie, 'Thomas Church and the Evolution of the Californian Garden', *Landscape Design*, London, February 1973, pp. 8–12.

23 Walker and Simo, *Invisible Gardens*, p. 99.

24 Eckbo, 'The basic aim should be recreation', pp. 18–20.

25 Griswold and Weller, *The Golden Age of American Gardens*, p. 199.

26 *Ibid.*, p. 263

27 *Ibid.*

28 Grant Carpenter Manson, *Frank Lloyd Wright to 1910: The First Golden Age*, 1958, p. 102.

29 The full story is told in M. Fulkerson and Ada Corson, *The Story of the Clearing*, Chicago Coach House Press, 1972.

30 Spirn, 'Frank Lloyd Wright, Architect of Landscape', p. 155.

31 *Ibid.*, p. 158.

masterwork**five**

roberto **burle marx**

1 William Howard Adams, *Roberto Burle Marx: The Unnatural Art of the Garden*, Museum of Modern Art/Abrams, New York, 1991, p. 40.

chapter**four**

1 James C. Rose, 'Freedom in the Garden', reprinted in *Pencil Points*, October 1938, in Treib (ed.), *Modern Landscape Architecture*, p. 70.

2 Maurice Maeterlinck, 'L'Intelligence des Fleurs', in *Life and Flowers*, trans. Alexander Teixeira de Mattos, London 1907, pp. 216–18, 235–36.

3 Wilfrid Blunt and William T. Stearn, *The Art of Botanical Illustration*, 1994 (revised ed.), p. 320.

4 Maggie Keswick, *The Chinese Garden, History, Art and Architecture*, 1978, p. 188.

5 Tunnard, *Gardens in the Modern Landscape*, pp. 120–25.

6 *Ibid.*, p. 87.

7 Eckbo, Kiley and Rose, 'Landscape Design for Urban Living', *Architectural Record*, May 1939, reprinted in Treib (ed.), *Modern Landscape Architecture*, p. 82.

8 Sylvia Crowe, *Garden Design*, 1958 ed., p. 114.

9 *Ibid.*, pp. 128–29.

10 *Ibid.*

11 John Nash, quotations from *The Artist Plantsman*, autobiographical essay, Anthony d'Offay, London, 1976; see also Sir John Rothenstein, *John Nash*, Macdonald, 1983.

12 Dr Gerd Daumel, *Concrete in the Garden*, trans. C. van Ameringen, Elsevier, 1971 (first published Düsseldorf 1963), pp. 9–10.

13 *Ibid.*, pp. 11–12.

14 Peter J. Bowler, *The Fontana History of the Environmental Sciences*, 1992, 'The origins of ecology', pp. 361–62.

15 Gert Groening and Joachim Wolschke-Bulmahn, 'Changes in the philosophy of garden architecture in the 20th century and their impact upon the social and spatial environment', in *Journal of Garden History, 1989*, vol. 9, no. 2, p. 54.

16 *Ibid.*, p. 56

17 The adoption of a 'Teutonic' natural landscape by the National Socialists is further explored in Joachim Wolschke-Buhlman, 'Teutonic Trends in Early Twentieth Century Landscape Design', in *Nature and Ideology: Natural Garden Design in the 20th Century,* Dumbarton Oaks Symposium, Washington, D.C., 20–21 May 1994.

18 Judith K. Major, review of *Nature and Ideology* symposium, on Jan Woudstra, 'Jac. P. Thijsse's Influence on Dutch Landscape Architecture', *Journal of Garden History*, vol. 15, no. 1, 1995, p. 63.

19 Groening and Wolschke-Buhlman, 'Changes in the philosophy of garden architecture', p. 54.

20 Thobjorn Andersson quoting Lorentz Bolin (1887–1972), 'Erik Glemme and the Stockholm Park System', in Treib (ed.), *Modern Landscape Architecture*, p. 118.

21 *Ibid.*, p. 121.

chapterfive

1 Sylvia Crowe, *Garden Design*, p. 73.

2 Russell Page, *The Education of a Gardener* (1983 ed.), illus. nos 46 and 47.

3 Geoffrey Jellicoe, 'The Studies of a Landscape Designer over Eighty Years', p. 16.

4 *Ibid.*, p. 32.

5 Frederick Gibberd, lecture given to the Royal Academy and the Institute of Landscape Architects, Marsh Lane papers.

6 *Ibid.*

chaptersix

1 Walker and Simo, *Invisible Gardens*, p. 215.

2 *Ibid.*, p. 203–4.

3 *Ibid.*, p. 209–11.

4 *Ibid.*, p. 211.

5 *Ibid.*, p. 216. The later chapters of Walker and Simo's book describe the rise of the corporate office.

6 C. C. McLaughlin (ed.), *The Papers of Frederick Law Olmsted*, John Hopkins University Press.

7 J. J. York, *Landscaping the American Dream, Gardens and Filmsets of Florence Yorke 1890–1972*, New York 1989.

8 See his biography *Ein Garten der Erinnerung*, by Eva Foerster and Gerhard Rostin, Berlin, 1982, p. 144.

9 See my *The Pursuit of Paradise* for an explanation of the rise of the small garden.

10 *Ibid.*, later chapters.

11 Spens, *Complete Landscape Designs and Gardens of Geoffrey Jellicoe*.

12 Page, *Education of a Gardener*, p. 85.

13 *Ibid.*

14 Jacques Wirtz, from G. Cooper and G. Taylor, *Paradise Transformed: The Private Gardening of the Twenty-First Century*, 1996, pp. 155–61; also *Les Jardins de Jacques Wirtz*, la Fondation pour l'architecture, Brussels, 1993.

15 Cooper and Taylor, *Paradise Transformed*, pp. 133–39.

16 Lodewijk Baljon, *Garden Design*, Spring 1999.

17 W. Oehme, James van Sweden and Susan R. Frey, *Bold Romantic Gardens: The New World Landscapes of Oehme and van Sweden*, Acropolis Books, Herndon VA, 1991.

18 Heidi Landecker (ed.), *Martha Schwartz, Transfiguration of the Commonplace*, Spacemaker Press, 1997.

19 Michael R. van Valkenburgh, Margaret Reeve, Jory Johnson, *Transforming the American Garden, Twelve New Landscape Designs*, Harvard University Graduate School of Design, 1986.

20 *Private Visions: The Gardens of Michael Van Valkenburgh*, Princeton Arch. Press, New York, 1994; review by Paula Dietz, *Harvard Graduate School of Design Review*, Spring 1995, p. 36.

21 Shodo Suzuki, quoted by Cooper and Taylor, *Paradise Transformed*, 1996, p. 45.

22 Gyorgy Kepes, *The New Landscape in Art and Science*, Paul Theobald, Chicago, 1956.

selectedreading

Adams, W. H., *Roberto Burle Marx: The Unnatural Art of the Garden*, New York, 1991

Allen, M. and S. Jellicoe, *The New Small Garden*, London, 1956

Benton, Charlotte, *A Different World: Emigré Architects in Britain 1928–1958*, London 1995

Benton, Tim, *The Villas of Le Corbusier 1920–1930*, London, 1987

Bingham, Neil, *Christopher Nicholson*, London, 1996

Brookes, John, *Room Outside*, London, 1964

———, *The New Small Garden Book*, London, 1992

Brown, Jane, and Richard Bryant, *A Garden and Three Houses: the story of Peter Aldington's garden and three village houses*, Woodbridge, Suffolk, 1999

———, *Eminent Gardeners*, London, 1990

———, *Lanning Roper and his gardens*, London, 1987

Church, Thomas D., Grace Hall, Michael Laurie, *Gardens Are for People*, New York, 1955 (republished 1983)

Cooper, Douglas and Guy Taylor, *Paradise Transformed*, London, 1996

Crowe, Sylvia, *Garden Design*, Woodbridge, Suffolk, 1958 (revised edition 1994)

Daumel, Gerd, *Concrete in the Garden*, Düsseldorf, 1963 (English edition 1971)

Eckbo, Garrett, *Landscape for Living*, New York 1950

———, *The Art of Home Landscaping*, New York, 1964

Imbert, Dorothée, *The Modernist Garden in France*, London, 1993

Jellicoe, Geoffrey, *Modern Private Gardens*, London, 1968

———, *The Studies of a Landscape Designer over Eighty Years* (vol. 1 of the *Collected Works*), Woodbridge, Suffolk, 1993

Kassler, Elizabeth B., *Modern Gardens and the Landscape*, New York, 1964

Kiley, Dan, and Jane Amidon, *Dan Kiley in His Own Words: America's Master Landscape Architect*, London, 1999

Landecker, H. (ed.), *Martha Schwartz: Transfiguration of the Commonplace*, Boston 1997

Lund, Annemarie, *Guide to Danish Landscape Architecture, 1000–1996*, Copenhagen 1997

Matteini, Milena, *Pietro Porcinai*, Milan, 1991

McGrath, Raymond, *The Twentieth Century House*, London, 1934

Neve, Christopher, *Unquiet Landscape: Places and Ideas in English 20th century painting*, London, 1990

Oehme, W., J. van Sweden and S. R. Frey, *Bold Romantic Gardens*, Reston, Virginia, 1990

Overy, Paul, *De Stijl*, London, 1991

Page, Russell, *The Education of a Gardener*, London, 1962 (reprinted)

Rispa, Raul (ed.), *Barragán: The Complete Works*, London, 1996

Shepheard, Peter, *Modern Gardens*, London, 1953

Schinz, M., and G. van Zuylen, *The Gardens of Russell Page*, New York, 1991

Spens, M., *The Complete Landscape Designs and Gardens of Geoffrey Jellicoe*, London, 1994

Taylor, C. G., *The Modern Garden*, London, 1936

Tojner and Vindum, *Arne Jacobsen, Architect and Designer 1902–1971*, Copenhagen 1991

Treib, M. (ed.), *Modern Landscape Architecture: A Critical Review*, London, 1993

The Twentieth Century Society, *The Modern House Revisited*, London, 1996

Walker, P. and M. Simo, *Invisible Gardens: The Search for Modernism in the American Landscape*, London, 1994

gazetteer

Not all of the gardens listed below are open to the public, and some are seasonally restricted. It is always advisable to make enquiries in advance.

Brazil

Sitio St Antonio da Bica (Roberto Burle Marx)
Campo Grande
Tel. 55 21 410 11 71

Ministry of Education (Roberto Burle Marx)
Palácio Capanema
Rio de Janeiro

Britain

St Catherine's College (Arne Jacobsen)
Oxford OX1 3UJ
Tel. 01865 271700
Group visits: please apply in writing to the Bursar

The Gibberd Garden (Sir Frederick Gibberd)
Marsh Lane
Gilden Way
Harlow
Essex CM17 0NA
Tel. 01279 442112

Denmans (John Brookes's garden)
Fontwell
Arundel
Sussex BN18 0SU
Tel. 01243 542808

Denmark

Arne Petersen's garden (Carl Theodor Sørensen):
Maleren Arne Petersen og Hustru Ebba Gregersens
Boliglegat
Randbølvej 13
Vanløse

Sonja Poll's garden (Carl Theodor Sørensen):
Kastanievej 16
Holte

Allotment gardens by Carl Theodor Sørensen:
Narumgårdsvej 73
Narum

Alice and Børge Mogensen's garden
(Morten Klint and Børge Mogensen)
Soløsevej 37
Gentofte

France

Villa Noailles (Gabriel Guevrekian)
Montée de Noailles
Hyères 83400
Tel. 04 94 35 90 00

Italy

Pietro Porcinai – contact:
Cassetta Postale 106
Ufficio postale di Firenze succursale 36
50135 Firenze

Holland

Tuin Mien Ruys
Moerheimstraat 78
7701 CG Dedemsvaart
Tel. 0523 614774

Mexico

Casa Luis Barragán
Francisco Ramirez 14
Col Daniel Garza
Mexico DF 11840
Tel. 525 515 49 08

USA

Naumkeag (Fletcher Steele)
Prospect Hill
Stockbridge
Massachusetts
Tel. 413 298 3239
www.thetrustees.org

Gropius House (Walter Gropius)
68 Baker Bridge Road
Lincoln
Massachusetts
Tel. 781 259 8098
www.spnea.org

PepsiCo Park (Russell Page)
Purchase
New York State

picture**credits**

88 From Peter Shepheard, *Modern Gardens*, 1953

89 The author

90 From M. Laurie, *An Introduction to Landscape Architecture*, 1976

91 Thomas D. Church Collection, Environmental Design Archives, University of California, Berkeley

92 From J. O. Simonds, *Landscape Architecture*, 1961

93 (top) From Sylvia Crowe, *Garden Design*, 1958; (middle and bottom) From Walker and Simo, *Invisible Gardens*, 1994, by kind permission

95 Museu de Arte de São Paulo, 1950

117 Author's collection

118 From R. McGrath, *Twentieth-Century Houses*, 1934

119 Scotts of Merriott, 1960

121 Architectural Association Photo Library (B. Housden)

122 From G. E. Kidder Smith, *Switzerland Builds*, Architectural Press, 1960

123 British Architectural Library, RIBA, London

124 S. R. Badmin, from *Trees for Town and Country*, 1947

125 By kind permission of Colvin and Moggridge

126 British Cement Association (formerly Cement and Concrete Association)

127 (above) © DACS London, 2000; (below) British Cement Association (Frank Newberry)

128–29 (plans) British Cement Association

128 (photos) The author

129 (photos) Dejardin Design

130 (top left, centre, bottom left) The author; (bottom right) Dejardin Design

131 (top) Dejardin Design; (centre left) The author; (centre right) The author's collection (Lanning Roper);

132 (centre) The author; (top and bottom) British Cement Association (George Perkin/Frank Newberry)

133 (top and centre) The author

154 The author

157 Geoffrey Jellicoe, author's collection

158–61 Vivian Russell

162 Lulu Salto Stephensen

163 Annemarie Lund

164 (top right) The author; (centre) British Cement Association (Frank Newberry)

165 (top and centre) Vivian Russell

188 The Office of Dan Kiley (Aaron Kiley)

192 James van Sweden

index

Page numbers in italic refer to illustrations

Aalto, Alvar 88, 134
Agnelli, Giovanni 136
America 81–97
Amsterdam 142, 193
Antwerp 142
Architectural Association 53, 158
Arp, Jean 19, 83, 94, 186, 193
Arthus University 176
Arts and Crafts 52
Ashmole, Professor Bernard 70

Bac, Ferdinand 194
Badmin, S. R. 124
Baljon, Lodewijk 193
Barr, Alfred H. Jr 82
Barragán, Luis 96, *164*, 194; El Pedregal, Mexico 194; Francisco Gilardi house, Mexico City 194; house and studio, Mexico City *195*; San Cristobal Stables, Mexico City *97, 195–99*
Barrett, Nathan 31
Bath, Marquess of 190
Battersea Pleasure Gardens, London 157, 189
Bauhaus 7, 9,12, 29, 50, 88
Bay Area, San Francisco 86, 94
Bayley Falbour, Sir Isaac 117
Bazeley, Geoffrey 54
Beaux Arts 12, 84, 86, 88, 188
Behrens, Peter 10, 11, 50
Beistegui, Comte Charles de 24
Benton, Tim 25
Bergin, Sylvia *117*, 118
Berkeley 85, 86, 88, 187
Berlin 25
Besant, Annie 18
Bijhouwer, Jan 142
Bingham, Neil 61, 62
Blom, Holger 64, 135
Bolin, Lorentz 135
Bordeaux 20
Boulogne-sur-Seine 21
Braekeleer, Henri de 191
Brandt, G. N. 163
Brazil 106–14
Breuer, Marcel 75, 86
Britain 49, 166
Bromley, Kent 70, *71*
Brown, Lancelot 'Capability' 9
Browne, Sir Thomas 61

Bullock, Alan 176
Bumpus, Judith 12
Bunney, M. J. H. and Charlotte 68
Burle Marx, Roberto 82, 96, 106–14, 116, 120, 124, 166, 189, 190, 193, 200; Flamengo Park, Rio de Janeiro *108*; garden for Odette Monteiro, Correias, Rio de Janeiro 106; garden for the Hospital da Lagoa (Sul America), Rio de Janeiro *113, 114*; Ministry of Education and Health, Rio de Janeiro *107*; roof garden of the Alfredo Schwarz house, Rio de Janeiro 106

Calder, Alexander 67
California 85, 86, 88, 94, 120, 187
California School 85, 86, 88
Cane, Percy 50, 66
Caneel-Claes, Jean 66, *66*, 67, *67*, 186
Caruncho, Fernando *192*, 193
Cement and Concrete Association, Wexham Springs, Buckinghamshire 126, *126*, *127*, *164*
Chadwick, Lynn 157
Chatto, Beth 122
Cheney, Mrs Edwin 13
Chermayeff, Serge 49, 53–54, 55, 57, 66; Bentley Wood, Halland, Sussex *56, 57*; De La Warr Pavilion, Bexhill, Sussex 54, *55*; Shrubswood, Chalfont St Giles, Buckinghamshire 53, *53*, 54, 186
Choate, Mabel 31
Church, Thomas 86, 88–94; *94*; Aptos garden, San Francisco 90, *91*; Donnell garden, Sonoma, 88, *88*, *89*, 90, *90, 91*; Kirkham garden *93*
CIRCLE 12
Clark, Frank 157
Clay, Eleanor 96
Coade, Eleanour 134
Collodi 166
Colvin, Brenda 23, 24, 122, 124, *125*, 155, 186, 187
Connell, Amyas 13; High and Over, Amersham, Bucks. *69*, 70
Constructivism 13, 58–61, 86
Copenhagen 176
Cornwall 59
Correvon, Fernand 117

Correvon, Henri 117–18, 120, 189; Lord Henry Bentinck's rock garden, Kirkby Lonsdale 117
Costa, Lucio 82, 106
Cranbrook Academy, Bloomfield Hills, Michigan *6, 11*
Creed, Henriette-Aimée 38
Crepin, Lucien 21
Crickmay, Colin 54
Crittall, Sir Francis 50
Crowe, Dr Warren 62
Crowe, Sylvia 60, 92, 122, 124, 155, *155*, 186, 187, 190; Town Garden, Wexham Springs *126, 127, 164*
Crowley, Mary B. 70
Cubism 24, 88
Cullen, Gordon 65, 119, 120
Curry, Bill 50

Daneway House, Cotswolds 53
Darmstadt 10
Dartington Hall, Devon 50
Daumel, Dr Gerd 134
De Stijl 12, 16–19, 90
Denmark 50, 163, 166
designers' plants 120–24
Dessau 72
Dillistone, George 142
Dobson, Frank 158
Donnell, Mr and Mrs Dewey 88
Dorn, Marion 52
Drachten, Friesland 16
Drury, Chris 191
Duchêne, Henri and Achille 24
Dymchurch 61

Eckbo, Garret 60, 82, 85–87, 88, 94, 98, 121, 122, 190; modern garden design *87*; pool garden, Beverly Hills, California *87*; sketch for 'Gardens and Gardening' annual *85*
ecological movement 135
Elliott, Clarence 61
Elmhirst, Leonard and Dorothy 50
Encke, Fritz 166
English landscape style 9
Etchells, Fredrick 20
Europe, post-war 155–63

Farrand, Beatrix 50
Festival of Britain 134, 156, 189
Fiesole 166
Florence 166
Foerster, Karl 156, 189

Ford, Edsel 96
'formes architecturales' 117–18, 120
Fox, Charles James 62
France 50
Froebel, Friedrich *12*, 13
Fry, Maxwell 49

Gabo, Naum 9, 13, 51, 58, 67, 82, 158, 193
gardens, Chinese 118–19; English 9, 119; French 31, 163; hanging 25; Italian 8, 163; Japanese 66, 119, 120; Mogul 8; plans analysis 68–71; prairie and desert 94–96; wild 134–35
Gardner, James 157
Garnier, Tony 50
Gartenschau 156
Gathorne-Hardy, Robert 127
Gaudier-Brzeska, Henri 158
George VI 53
Germany 166, 193
Gerns, Ludwig 193, 200, *201–8*
Gerona 191
Gesellius 10
Gibberd, Frederick 158–62, *165*; 187; Heathrow Airport 159; InterContinental Hotel, Hyde Park Corner, London 159; Kielder Reservoir, Northumberland 159; Marsh Lane, Old Harlow, Essex *133*, 134, *158*, 159, *159, 160, 161, 164, 165*, 186; Roman Catholic Cathedral, Liverpool 159
Giedion, Siegfried 12, 134, 193
Gill, Eric 158
Girard, Alexander 98
Giverny 120
Glemme, Erik 135; Blossom Garden, Tegner Grove 135; Vasa Park 135
Goldsworthy, Andy 191
Gorrara, Mary *161*
Greene, Lord Justice Wilfred 52
Gropius, Ise 72
Gropius, Walter 8–9, 10, 11, 12, 26, 49–50, 62, 72–80, *79*, 81, 82, 86, 121, 156, 186, 187, 193; Gropius house, Lincoln 72–80, *74–80*, 95
Guevrekian, Gabriel 38; garden at Villa Noailles, Hyères 38, *39–47*
Guggenheim, Peggy 67

Haefeli, Max 122
Haifa 54

Halprin, Lawrence 13, 92, 124
Hamilton Finlay, Ian 191
Hampton, Anthony 127
Hanover 200
Harkness, Sarah P. 81
Harlow new town 158, 159
Harvard 72, 82, 85, 86, 98, 187, 188, 189, 193
Harvey, J. D. M. 53
Helsingfors 10
Hemel Hempstead 158
Hepworth, Barbara 58, 59–60, 186; *Archaen*, St Catherine's Oxford *179*; studio and garden, St Ives, Cornwall 59, *59*
Hidcote Manor, Gloucestershire 191
High Modern Movement 8
Hill, Oliver 13, 52–53; Frinton Park Estate, Essex 53; Holthanger, Wentworth Estate, Surrey *51*, 53; Joldwynds, Holmbury St Mary, Surrey *51*, 52
Hitchcock, Henry Russell 82
Hitchens, Ivon 159
Hoffman, Josef 38
Holland 16–19, 193
Holme, Charles 120
Houzik, Karel 115
Hudnut, Dean Joseph 82, 84
Hussey, Christopher 9, 13
Hvittrask 10, 96
Hyères 38

Imbert, Dorothée 13, 20, 21
Impressionists 12
Institute of Landscape Architects 50, 51, 190
International Federation of Landscape Architects 156, 157
International Modern Movement 8
Internationalism 8
Israel 55

Jacobsen, Arne *132*; 186; Arthus University 176; Munkegard Elementary School, Vangede, Denmark 176, *162*; Rodovre town hall 176; St Catherine's, Oxford 176, *176–84*
Japan 119, 193
Jeanneret, Pierre 19, 20
Jeanneret, Charles-Edouard see Le Corbusier

Jekyll, Gertrude 52, 124, 142, 156, 189
Jellicoe, Geoffrey 12, 13, 51, 53, 68–69, 156, 157–58, 187, 190, 193; Church Hill Memorial garden, Walsall 158; roof garden, Harvey's store, Guildford 157; rose garden, Cliveden, Buckinghamshire *156*; Royal Lodge, Windsor 53; Shute House, Wiltshire *157*, 190; Sutton Place, Surrey 190; Terrace Garden *128–29*
Jellicoe, Susan 13, 68–69, 126, *128–29*
Jensen, Jens 13, 96, 188
Johnson, Hugh 162
Johnson, Philip 82
Jorgensen, Erstad 163; playground, Emdrup 163

Kandinsky, Vasily 19, 67, 94, 186
Kassler, Elizabeth B. 13
Keene, Sir Charles 70
Kemp family 71
Kennington, Eric 158
Kent, William 84
Kepes, Gyorgy 193
Ketting, Piet 17
Kiley, Dan 82, 86, 98, 121, 122; Gregory house, Wayzata, Minnesota 98; Kimmel residence, Salisbury, Connecticut *188*; Kusko house, Williamstown, Massachusetts 98; Lear residence, Brentwood, California 98; Lehr residence, Miami Beach, Florida 98; Miller House, Columbus, Indiana 98–105, *99–105, 133*; Philosopher's garden, Rockefeller University, New York 98
Klee, Paul 12, 15, 19, 29, 58, 67, 156, 186; *Plan for a Garden 29*, 29
Kok, Antony 16
Kyoto 119

Lancaster, Osbert 157
Lange, Willy 135
Lao Chou 118
Larissa 26
Laurie, Michael 88

Le Corbusier 9, 11, 12, 15, 19–25, 68, 81, 98, 118, 186, 190; Beistegui roof garden 24; Immeuble-Villas 19; *Pavilion de l'Esprit Nouveau* 19, 20; Ternisien House project 21, *21*; Villa Les Terrasses, Garches *20*, 21, 68; Villa Meyer *22*; Villa Savoye, Poissy 25
Le Nôtre, André 163, 190, 191
Leach, Bernard 119
Leeds Castle 136
Legrain, Pierre-Emile 200
Lescaze, William 50; High Cross House, Dartington 50
Lindgren 10
Liverpool, Roman Catholic Cathedral 159
London 38, 160; 13 Downshire Hill, Hampstead 68, *68*; No. 19 Grove Terrace, Highgate 68, *69*; InterContinental Hotel, Hyde Park Corner 159
Long Island 82
Long, Richard 191
Longleat 136
Loos, Adolf 38, 66, 115
Lubetkin, Berthold 38, 58
Lucas, Colin *121*
Lutyens, Edwin 51, 89; Tyringham Hall 134
Lynch, Kevin 13

Maas, Luise 25
MacCarter, Robert 12
Mackinosh Charles Rennie 10, 117
Maeterlinck, Maurice 115–16, 118
Mallet-Stevens, Robert 38, 41
Manning, Warren 98
MARS Group 62, *63*, 66
Marsan, Signora Ajmone 136
Martin, Leslie 50–51
Mattern, Hermann 156
Maybeck, Bernard 88
McGrath, Raymond 13, 62–63; Land's End, Gaulby, Leicestershire 70, *70*; St Ann's Hill, Chertsey, Surrey *48*, 62–65, 134
Mendelsohn, Erich 9, 11–12, 15, 19, 25–28, 49, 53–55, 68, 111, 166; 'am Rupenhorn', Berlin 26, 27, *27*, 28, *28*, 53, 186; De La Warr Pavilion, Bexhill, Sussex 54, *55*; Einstein Tower 26; Mount Carmel garden city design 26; Shrubswood,

Chalfont St Giles, Buckinghamshire 53, *53*, 54, 186; Schocken commissions 26, 53; Weizmann garden, Reheboth, Tel-Aviv 26, *27*
Meyer, Mr and Mrs Ulrich 193
Miall family 71
Mies van der Rohe, Ludwig 10, 11, 81, 82, 196; Farnsworth House, Plano, Illinois 25
Miller, Irwin 98
Miller, Wilhelm 96
Milles, Carl 7, 10, 11, 50
Miró, Joan 67, 94
modernism 8, 26, 50, 81, 106, 188, 193, 200
Moholy-Nagy, Lázló 13, 51, 58, 94, 186
Moller, Jonna 176
Mondrian, Piet 15, 16, 17, 18–19, 58–59, 142, 186, 196; *Tableau I, Composition with Red, Black, Blue and Yellow 18*
Monet, Claude 12, 120
Monier, Joseph 134
Monzie, Gabrielle de 21
Moore, Henry 12, 57, 58, 60, 67, 158, 186, 190; *Recumbent Figure* 57, *57*, 60; *Seated Woman 100, 103*
Morandi, Riccardo 166
Moreux, Jean-Charles 24
Morgan, Julia 88
Mortimer, Raymond 66
Mumford, Lewis 13
Munich 25
Muntz, Elizabeth 158
Nash, John 58, 61, 126–27
Nash, Paul 58, 61, 67, 83
Neutra, Richard 26, 84; plan for the Nesbitt house and garden, Brentwood, California *95*
Neve, Christopher 61
New York 19, 82
Nicholson, Basil D. 21
Nicholson, Ben 19, 51, 58–59, 61, 159
Nicholson, Christopher (Kit) 61–62, 63; greenhouse design, Kit's Close, Fawley, Green, Oxfordshire *61, 62, 62*; studio for Augustus John, Fryern Court, Hampshire 61, 62
Niemeyer, Oscar 82, 106
Nimmo, R. L. 53
Noailles, Charles de 38

Ocampo, Victoria 26
Oehme, Wolfgang 193; garden for Mr and Mrs Ulrich Meyer, Lake Michigan *192*
Olmsted, Frederick Law 13, 84, 88, 98, 188, 189
Olbricht, Josef 10
Otterlo 17
Oud, J. J. P. 15, 16–17, 81; blocks at Tussendijken, Rotterdam 16

Page, Russell 157, 189, 190–91, 193, 200; PepsiCo headquarters, Purchase, New York state 136; Villa Silvio Pellico, Turin 136, *136–41*, 157, 190
Paley, William S. 81
Palle-Schmidt, J., water court at Lyngby Training Centre, Lyngby, Denmark *163*
Pares, Susan see Jellicoe, Susan
Paris 19, 38, 190, 200
paving *132–33*
Paxton, Sir Joseph 115
Peking 118
Picasso, Pablo 58, 158, 186
Picturesque 9, 25, 65
Pilkington Glass 52
Piper, John 157
plants 115–31, 189; designers' plants 120–24
Porcinai, Pietro 157, 186, 200; Giardino della Società Nariana, Fiesole, Florence *116*; Villa Il Roseto, Florence 166, *166–75*; Villa L'Imperialino, Florence 166
Portofino 166
postmodernism 7, 136
prairie gardens 96
Pritchard, Jack and Molly 49
Pryde, Mabel 59
Pulham, James 134
Read, Herbert 58, 59
Repton, Humphry 8, 189
Rienks de Boer, Cornelis 16
Rietveld, Gerrit 15, 16, 17; Pavilion, Kroller-Muller Museum 17; Schroeder house 17
Rio de Janeiro 106
Robert, Philippe 117
Robertson, Mary 'Bob' 67
Robinson, William 156, 189
Roche, Kevin 98
Rockrise, George 88

Rodovre 176
Roper, Lanning 190
Rose, James 82, 86, 98, 115, 121, 122, 189
Rotterdam 16
Royston, Robert 87; Naify garden, Woodside, California 93
Rubinstein, Gerda 164
Ruys, Mien 17, 118, 124, 135, 186, 187, 189, 200, 164, 165; Dedemsvaart, Netherlands 132, 133, 134, 142, 142–54, 187

Sa Torre Cega, Majorca 136
Saarinen, Eero 10, 98
Saarinen, Eliel 7, 8–11, 96; Molchow-Haus, Viborg 10
Sackville-West, Vita 52
Samuel, Godfrey 70
San Francisco 28, 88
Sasaki, Hideo 188, 189
Scarpa, Carlo 166
Schlesinger, G.L. 64
Schocken department store 26
Schwartz, Martha 193; Bagel garden, Boston 193
Scotts' Nurseries 119
Segal, Walter 9
Shephard-Parpagliolo, Maria 157
Shepheard, Peter 13; Moat Garden, Festival of Britain 123, 156
Shepherd, J. H. 158
Shin style 119
Silver End, Essex 50
Simo, Melanie 13
Simonds, J. O. 92
Sissinghurst Castle, Kent 191
So style 119
Sørensen, Carl Theodor 176, 187; Ordrup 163
Soukop, Willi 63
Spain 191, 193
Spankkova, Ingermanland 9
Spirn, Anne Whiston 13, 96
St Petersburg 9
Steele, Fletcher 30, 82, 90, 188; Naumkeag, Stockbridge, Massachusetts 14, 30, 31–37, 82, 193
Stein, Michael 20
Stockholm 10
'Stockholm School' 134–35
Stoke Bishop, Bristol, Orchard House 71

Storrow, Mrs James 75
Strasbourg 17
Stratford-upon-Avon 159
Stroud, Dorothy 9
Stuttgart 16
Su Hua 118
Sunset school, California 134
Suzuki, Shodo 193
Swanson, Robert 10
Sweden 50, 135
Synge, Patrick M. 126

Taylor, G. C. 13
Teheran 38
Tewin, Hertfordshire 70, 71
Thijsse, Jacobus Pieter 135
Thomas, R. N. 70
Thoreau, Henry David 98
Tor Lorenzo, Rome 136
Trevor-Roper, Patrick 26
Tschichold, Jan 17
Tunnard, Christopher 55, 57, 62–63, 65–67, 70, 82–84, 118, 119, 121, 142, 189, 190; Bentley Wood, Halland, Sussex 56, 57; garden for 4 Buckingham Street, Cambridge, Massachusetts 83; Land's End, Gaulby, Leicestershire 70, 70; plan for a garden at Newport, Rhode Island 83, 83; St Ann's Hill, Chertsey, Surrey 48, 62–65, 64, 65, 134
Tunnard, John 66, 67
Tunnard, Viola 66
Tussendijken, Rotterdam 16
Tyrwhitt, Jacqueline 124
Tzu Hsi, Empress 118

Underwood, Leon 165
Utrecht 17

Valentien, Otto plan for a small garden in Stuttgart 118
Van Doesburg, Theo 15, 16, 17, 142; Theo Drachten housing scheme 16; Garden Sculpture 16, 17
van Sweden, James 193; garden for Mr and Mrs Ulrich Meyer, Lake Michigan 192
van Valkenburgh, Michael 193
Vangede 176
Velde, Henry van der 28
Vera, André and Paul 24, 50, 200; Côte Jardin, Paris 23; garden at St

Germain-en-Laye 24; garden for Jacques Rouché, Paris 23
Viborg, Finland 10
Vienna 38
Vilmorin, André de 190

Walker, Peter 13
Walton, Sir William 136
Washington, D.C. 193
Webb, Philip 52
White, Stanley 188
Wiebe, Edward 12
Williams, Edward A. 87
Wils, Jan 17
Windsor, Duke of 136
Wirtz, Jacques 191
Wirtz, Martin and Peter 191
Wood-Roper, Laura 189
Wright, Frank Lloyd 12–13, 26, 52, 96; Conley House 96; Sherman M. Booth house 96; Taliesin West 13, 96; Thomas Hardy House 13

Yamoaka, Mr 119
Yoch, Florence 189
Yorke, F. R. S. 13
Young, Monica 159

Zion and Breen Associates, Paley Park, East 53rd Street, New York 81

First published in the United Kingdom in 2000 by
Thames & Hudson Ltd, 181A High Holborn, London WC1V 7QX

www.thamesandhudson.com

© 2000 Thames & Hudson Ltd, London

First paperback edition 2001
Reprinted 2002

British Library Cataloguing-in-Publication Data
A catalogue record for this book is available from the British Library

ISBN 0-500-28321-4

Printed and bound in China by C. S. Graphics